Britain
1890–1939

Rosemary Rees

Series Editors
Martin Collier
Rosemary Rees

HEINEMANN ADVANCED HISTORY

Heinemann is an imprint of Pearson Education Limited,
a company incorporated in England and Wales,
having its registered office at Edinburgh Gate, Harlow
CM20 2JE. Registered company number: 872828

Heinemann is a registered trademark of Pearson Education Limited

© Rosemary Rees, 2003

First published 2003

10
10 9 8 7 6

ISBN: 978 0 435327 57 6

Designed, illustrated and typeset by Wyvern 21 Ltd

Original illustrations © Harcourt Education Limited 2003

Printed in China (CTPS/06)

Index compiled by Ian D Crane

Photographic acknowledgements

The author and publisher would like to thank the following for permission to
reproduce photographs:

Cover photograph: © Punch

page 2, Illustrated London News; page 16, Topham Picturepoint; page 22,
Corbis; page 26, Punch; page 32, source unknown; page 54, Museum of London;
page 60, Hulton; page 68, Punch; page 71, Punch; page 79, Imperial War
Museum; page 83, Hulton Archive; page 98, Hulton; page 107, Punch; page 119,
Punch; page 130, Hulton Archive; page 132, Punch; page 141, Topham;
page 152, Hulton Archive; page 160, source unknown; page 163, Hulton Archive;
page 164, Daily Express.

Dedication

This book is dedicated to the family with whom it began. In particular it is
dedicated to Agnes, my grandmother, and Alice and Rose, my two great-aunts.

CONTENTS

HOW TO USE THIS BOOK

This book is divided into two distinct sections.

The AS section describes and explains the main economic, social and political developments in Britain between 1890 and 1939. The text of this narrative aims to give the student in-depth information and some basic analysis. The summary questions at the end of each chapter challenge the student to use the information to explain, evaluate and analyse important aspects of the topic covered by that chapter. In this way, students will acquire a clear understanding of the key features of each topic.

The A2 section focuses on the decline of the Liberal Party during this period and is more analytical in style. It also focuses on the main theories that seek to explain the collapse of the party, both in Parliament and in the country, from the heady days of 1906 to the wilderness years of the 1920s. Students who use this section should refer back to the relevant AS chapters that provide the factual underpinning to the debates.

At the end of each section, there is an Assessment section. The AS Assessment section is based on the requirements of the three Awarding Bodies – AQA, Edexcel (London Qualifications) and OCR – and gives students detailed guidance on how to answer the questions set. The A2 Assessment section is based on the requirements of Edexcel for its synoptic Unit 6 paper 'The Decline of the Liberal Party, c.1900–29'.

The bibliography suggests the mainstream books that students may wish to consult. It also gives a selection of documentary readings, together with suggestions about appropriate contemporary accounts and relevant fiction. Students are strongly advised to broaden their understanding of the period by reading as widely as possible.

AS SECTION: NARRATIVE AND EXPLANATION

INTRODUCTION: PEOPLE AND POWER

WHO WERE THE PEOPLE?

What was it like to have been alive in the Britain of 1890? Let us start with a real family, living in London ten years before the nineteenth century ended.

The Crane family of Islington, London, in 1890

In 1890, Alice Crane was twelve years old; her brother Henry was ten; her younger sister Agnes was seven; and Rose, the baby, was just one year old. Their father, George, was a drayman, working for a local brewery driving a horse-drawn cart and delivering barrels of beer to public houses in and around King's Cross. In the evenings, he helped out at the pub on the corner of Barnsbury Road, where the family lived. Their mother Martha took in sewing, patching, darning and mending as well as making shirts and aprons, dresses and pinafores for local people. The family lived mainly in the basement and on the ground floor of their rented house. Three rooms on the first floor were let out to a variety of lodgers, while 'poor aunt Lizzie' lived in the two big attic rooms with her 'come-by-chance' daughter Kitty – the result of a weekend fling in Margate. There was nothing remarkable about this young family, struggling to make a living in the sprawling, busy, noisy, prosperous, filthy city that was London. But in what sort of a Britain were they trying to make their way? What were their chances of survival or even of prosperity?

A new London?

George and Martha, when they had the time, had a good social life. There was always the pub where George worked, but it wasn't thought suitable for respectable women to be seen in pubs, even when their husbands were there. When George and Martha could manage an evening out, Kitty would baby-sit for them and they would go to the music halls. George liked to bet on the dogs and Martha went 'up West' with Kitty to see the lights and window shop in Oxford Street and Regent Street. There was a sense of newness and excitement about life in London in the 1890s.

- Cheap electricity meant electric street lighting and, from 1900, electric trams.
- The first cars were seen on the streets; a speed limit of 4 miles per hour was raised to a dangerous 12 mph in 1896.

London itself was growing and spreading.

- Most of London's over-ground rail network was electrified in the 1890s as was the underground, begun in the 1860s and running deep beneath the streets.

- The thriving business centre of London created thousands of new jobs in the 1890s and the creation of an efficient transport network meant that these new 'white collar' workers could live further and further away from their work places. The middle classes, and those aspiring to the middle class, opted for a life in the leafy suburbs and commuting to work.

Martha and George, however, could not afford to move out of London. They, and thousands of families like them, had to stay close to the breadwinner's place of work. Gradually, only the poorest workers remained living in the centre of London and other large cities.

Life chances

The life chances that the girls Alice, Agnes and Rose had were far greater and more varied than those of their mother when she was a child. Martha hadn't attended any school at all, but had taught herself to read and write from her children's schoolbooks. In 1890 Alice and Agnes were attending the local **board school**; Rose went there four years later.

- The 1880 Education Act made elementary education (5–10 year olds) compulsory for all children. In 1891 elementary education was made free.
- Secondary education was different. Here, girls and the parents of girls had to fight hard to get the kind of education that was considered to be the right of middle-class boys. But change was coming. The North London Collegiate School, founded in 1850 in Camden Town, London, for 'young ladies' was flourishing by the 1890s and had spawned many similar establishments. They remained for many years, however, the province of the middle classes.
- Most working-class children finished their education at elementary school, where in 1880 the school-leaving age was ten for good attenders or thirteen years for those with too few registered attendances. It wasn't until 1918 that the school-leaving age was raised to fourteen.

Compulsory school attendance pushed literacy rates up to around 95 per cent and the 1890s were characterised by increasing membership of libraries and a proliferation of romantic and adventurous fiction that was produced quickly and cheaply. Reading at home after work became increasingly popular as, by the end of the century, most homes had gas light.

And what of Henry? Henry, a sickly weak-chested child, went to the board school with his sisters. At the age of twelve he was, with some reluctance on the part of his parents, apprenticed to an upholsterer. There, the dust from the horsehair, the chemicals from the leather and dyestuffs from heavy cloth affected his already diseased lungs. He died from tuberculosis (TB) in 1901, two days before his 21st birthday.

- TB probably accounted for one-third of all deaths in the nineteenth century although its incidence lessened as the century progressed.
- TB hit all classes, but it hit hardest the working classes who had poor nutrition and lived or worked in overcrowded, badly ventilated conditions.

Henry's family, along with 5 million other working-class families, paid a small weekly sum into a **friendly society**. This paid out a death benefit (it was enough to bury Henry) and small sums to help meet the cost of calling a doctor on very rare occasions.

The world of work ...

Job opportunities for girls opened up considerably in the 1890s. Alice and Agnes worked as seamstresses, learning to handle the relatively new treadle sewing machines so that they could sew flat and French seams, smock and frill, set sleeves and make buttonholes. Rose, always the odd one out, went to work in a fancy goods factory.

By the 1890s, girls and young women were working as secretaries and telephonists, shop assistants and filing clerks. Able working-class girls could become elementary school teachers and so pull themselves into the ranks of the lower middle class. The doors to universities were beginning to creak open and medicine, the law and academic work were slowly becoming career possibilities

KEY ORGANISATION

Friendly society Workers paid a small weekly contribution to friendly societies. In return, they were provided with sickness and funeral benefits. By 1890, about 80 per cent of the adult male population were members of a friendly society. Governments were fairly ambivalent towards them. They encouraged them as examples of self-help, but were suspicious of them as independent working-class organisations.

Angel in the House A man called Coventry Patmore wrote a long poem called *The Angel in the House*. In it he said that women were 'angels' at home, full of love and kindness and caring for others. Men, on the other hand, were good at doing things, taking responsibility and making decisions. These ideals led to the belief that a woman's place was in the 'private' sphere of the home, and a man's place was in the 'public' sphere of work.

for the clever and determined. Even so, the 1891 census revealed that 11.6 per cent of the total female population of England and Wales were employed as domestic servants.

Most young women, though, had to give up working when they married. The idea of the **Angel in the House** was not quite dead: husbands were still supposed to be the breadwinners for wife and family. While this may have been the dream, it certainly was not the reality.

In 1890:

- women made up around 29 per cent of the national work force
- 55 per cent of single women worked outside the home
- 30 per cent of widows worked outside the home
- 10 per cent of married women worked outside the home.

The proportions varied from region to region. In the cotton manufacturing districts of Lancashire, for example, women made up around 60 per cent of the workforce. On the other hand, ship-building and mining areas, like the north-east of England, provided far fewer opportunities for women workers.

Women were among the most vulnerable members of the workforce. Generally younger and less skilled than the men, they were the first to be laid off when times were bad. But, from about 1890, female membership of trade unions grew at the same rate as trade unionism as a whole. Women became as vociferous as men in demanding their rights.

In 1890, Martha, the mother of Alice and Henry, Agnes and Rose, took in lodgers and sewing in order to help the family budget and to make ends meet. Millions of married women adopted similar expedients to Martha, for example child-minding, taking in washing, and selling home-cooked food in their front rooms. This was a largely hidden and unquantifiable workforce. Millions more women undertook piece work at home for a variety of operators: making buttons, for example, where they could earn a pittance but combine it with their domestic responsibilities such as childcare. Countless families were saved from real hardship in this way.

... and of marriage

Martha and George married on Christmas Day 1876. The legal niceties of who could possess what after their marriage didn't much bother them as they both owned so little and nothing of any value. But earlier in the century, everything a woman possessed became her husband's when she married. In fact, the woman herself was regarded very much as being her husband's possession, to do with as he chose. Times, however, were changing.

- In 1870, the first Married Women's Property Act allowed women to keep their own earnings from employment after marriage.
- The 1882 Married Women's Property Act allowed women to keep any property they owned before their marriage, have the same rights over their property as if they were unmarried, and allowed wives to carry on trades and businesses using their own property.

It was different where women, children and divorce were concerned. While it was possible to divorce, a man wanting to divorce his wife had to prove her adultery; a woman wanting to divorce her husband had to prove not only his adultery, but incest, bigamy, cruelty or desertion as well.

- In 1886, the Married Women (Maintenance in Case of Desertion) Act allowed deserted women to sue their husbands for maintenance before becoming so destitute they had to enter the workhouse.
- In the same year, the Guardianship of Infants Act stipulated that the needs of children had to be taken into account before deciding which parent should have custody after a divorce.
- In 1891, the law decreed that a man could not force his wife to live in the matrimonial home.

Gradually, the law recognised the rights of married women. Separation and divorce were all on the increase in the 1890s, but the numbers remained very small. Death was by far the most common reason for marriages to end. Because death rates fell more for women than for men, many women were widowed and did not re-marry. This surplus of women over men increased steadily between 1871 and 1911. Maybe the two elder Crane girls were in a hurry. They certainly married younger than most of their age group. Alice married in 1900 when she was 22, and Agnes in 1904 when she was 21. Rose, different as always, never married.

WHO HAD THE POWER?

The basis of power

The basis of power in 1890 was the ownership of land. Roughly 10 per cent of the adult British population owned 95 per cent of the land. This land wasn't just farming land, but land on which the great streets and squares of London – Regent Street and Bedford Square, for example – were built. Docks and ports, ironworks and mines were mostly privately owned and the owners wielded power, too. Power, therefore, was concentrated in the hands of a few men, who used it for good or ill. Some great landowners chose to remain aloof from politics, developing their own estates and interests. Most, however, could not resist the temptation to wield power on a larger stage and entered the world of politics. Here, political power was divided between the House of Lords, the House of Commons and the Crown, though not in equal measure.

The House of Commons

Political parties were well established and organised by 1890, with the Conservative and Liberal parties dominating the parliamentary scene. Even so, edges were sometimes blurred and it wasn't unknown for individuals to switch parties at crucial times. **Joseph Chamberlain**, for example, left the Liberal Party in 1886, was fully accepted by the Conservatives and led the Tory Colonial Office in 1895.

The basis of any government's power was (and still is) its ability to command a majority in the House of Commons,

KEY PERSON

Joseph Chamberlain (1836–1914) Chamberlain made his fortune in Birmingham as a manufacturer of screws. He made Birmingham his power base and, as mayor 1873–5, he introduced many social reforms, including improvements in public health and housing. Elected Liberal MP for Birmingham in 1876, he served under Gladstone as President of the Board of Trade 1880–5, but broke with him in 1886 over Ireland. He crossed over to the Conservative and Unionist Party and became colonial secretary in Salisbury's government of 1895–1902. He resigned from Balfour's Conservative government in 1903 to campaign for 'imperial preference' rather than free trade. Many historians believe that the divisions which this led to brought about the Liberal landslide victory in 1906.

and this majority was won at general elections. Provided their majority held up, a government could stay in power for seven years, although in practice general elections were held more frequently. In the 1890s, there were general elections in 1892 and 1895, with a further one in 1900. You can see the results of these in the grid on page 11.

Who could vote in general elections? In 1890, no woman could vote in a general election. Matters of government and national security were, it was believed by most people, best left to the men. But by no means was there universal male suffrage.

- The 1867 Parliamentary Reform Act gave the vote in county seats to:
  - men owning, or having leases longer than sixty years, for land valued at £5 per year
  - men occupying land with a rateable value of £12 a year, provided they had paid their poor rates
  and in the boroughs to:
  - men owning, or occupying, dwelling houses for at least twelve months
  - male lodgers in houses worth at least £10 a year and who had lived there for at least twelve months.
- In 1884, most constituencies became single-member constituencies. Borough and county franchises were made the same.

By 1890, there were approximately 5.7 million voters: about six men from every ten were entitled to elect members of Parliament. George Crane was one of them. Martha, of course, was not.

The House of Lords

Dukes and earls, marquises and bishops sat in the House of Lords. Most were great landowners and many, although sympathising with the Liberals or Conservatives on specific issues, were not members of any particular political party. Some, of course, were highly politicised. Lord Salisbury, leader of the Conservative Party and Prime Minister for much of the 1890s, sat in the House of Lords, and this was not thought in any way odd or peculiar. However,

- propertied interests and Peers in the House of Lords began to rally more and more behind the Conservatives with the result that they could block Liberal legislation when the Liberals were in a majority in the Commons and formed the government;
- by 1890, it was becoming clear that the Liberals could, if they so wished, rally popular support in the Commons and outside, against the House of Lords and its privileges. There was a fine balance to be kept and one that David Lloyd George exploited to the full twenty years later.

The Crown

Queen Victoria came to the throne in 1837 and by 1890 had eleven years still to reign. Her main constitutional role, insofar as wielding political power was concerned, was to choose the prime minister. In practice, however, Victoria's power to do this was diminishing.

- Party organisation and discipline meant that her 'choice' was almost inevitably limited to the leader of the party that commanded a majority in the Commons.
- Increasingly querulous, bad-tempered and partisan, she found this erosion of her power impossible to understand and hard to cope with. The Conservatives, traditionalist by nature and inclination, accepted without much of a murmur Victoria's choice of Lord Salisbury as prime minister over the more perceptive Sir Stafford Northcote
- The Liberals, with their tendency to mild radicalism, blocked her attempts to persuade Lord Granville and then Lord Hartington to form a Liberal government when William Gladstone, whom she disliked intensely, was the undisputed leader of the Liberal Party. Nevertheless, throughout his time as Prime Minister, Victoria did all she could to undermine him.

Votes for women?

The voting restrictions on women only applied to general elections, and even here, in 1890, there was pressure for change.

- In 1890, there were various suffrage movements demanding the vote for women. But, at a time when not

all men had the vote, who would seriously consider giving it to all women?
- Between 1870 and 1914, no fewer that 28 Women's Suffrage bills came before Parliament. They all failed.

Many believed that the proper sphere within which women should exercise their influence was the domestic one. Gradually this belief extended to allowing women to participate in local politics because of the impact they had on domestic matters.

- In 1869, the Municipal Franchise Act extended the vote to women ratepayers in local elections
- The Education Act of 1870 allowed women to vote for the new school boards, and also to be elected to serve on them.
- In 1875, women could be elected as Poor Law guardians (women ratepayers had been able to vote for guardians from 1834).
- In 1888, the Local Government Act permitted women to vote for new county and borough councils.
- In 1894 the Parish Councils Act permitted women to serve on urban and district councils.

In the 1890s, it is clear that some determined women were exercising considerable authority in education administration and local government.

Martha and her daughters Alice and Agnes had to wait until 1918 before they could vote in general elections. By then, Martha was 70 years old, Alice was 40 and Agnes 36. Rose, just too young in 1918, had to wait until 1928 when she was 39 years old. 'Politics,' Rose declared in later life, 'ain't for the likes of me.'

HEINEMANN ADVANCED HISTORY

CHAPTER 1

Why did the Liberal Party win the general election of 1906?

Britain was governed by the Conservative Party for most of the 1890s and for the first five years of the twentieth century. In each general election, the Conservatives had a cosiderable majority. However, in 1906 the situation was reversed. The Liberal Party swept to power in a landslide victory. Why did this happen?

	1886		1892		1895		1900		1906	
	%	Seats	%	Seats	%	Seats	%	Seats	%	Seats
Conservative	51.4	393	47.0	313	49.1	411	50.3	402	43.4	156
Liberal	45.0	192	45.1	272	45.7	177	45.0	183	49.4	399
Irish Nationalist	3.5	85	7.0	81	4.0	82	2.6	82	0.7	86
Labour	0	0	0	0	0	0	1.3	2	4.8	29
Other	0.1	0	0.9	4	0.2	0	0.8	1	1.7	4

General election results, 1886–1906

HOW HAD THE CONSERVATIVE PARTY RETAINED POWER 1886–1906?

At the end of the nineteenth and beginning of the twentieth centuries, politics was dominated by two great political parties: the Conservative Party and the Liberal Party. By 1906, the Conservatives had been in power for eleven years. They had won the general elections of 1886, 1895 and 1900 because of the following:

- The Conservative Party deliberately began to adapt its policies so that it appealed to the new, urban middle class and to working-class voters. Before the 1880s, the Conservative Party was associated with traditional values: land, the gentry and agriculture. In repositioning itself, the Conservative Party began to appeal to those who previously supported the Liberal Party.

- The 1884–5 Reform Acts created small, single-member constituencies. This meant that pockets of urban middle-class Conservative voters were not swamped by other voters.
- In the 1880s, the Conservatives developed an efficient party machine, with professional agents and centrally produced propaganda material. In 1900, for example, there were 30 Conservative agents working in London and only three Liberal ones.
- **Robert Cecil, Lord Salisbury**, was a skilful leader of the Party.

However, for the Conservative Party, cataclysmic change was to come, as the general election results show. What had happened to destroy the parliamentary Conservative Party?

WAS THE GENERAL ELECTION OF 1906 LOST BECAUSE OF MISTAKES MADE BY THE CONSERVATIVE GOVERNMENT?

In the 1890s, the Liberal Party was in the wilderness. Its leaders were divided about their aims and objectives. Most of its finances had gone with the Liberal **Unionists** to the Conservative Party. The Liberals had little money to mobilise resources and supporters in election campaigns. Many Liberal organisations in the country at large had withered and died. Among those who still supported liberalism and the basic ideals of the Liberal Party, there was a distinct lack of morale. Against this background, the Liberal landslide victory in 1906 looks startling. We must therefore look to the Conservative government for the beginning, at least, of an explanation.

Was the Boer War responsible?
The Boer War (1899–1902) was part of an attempt by the British government to reimpose its control on southern Africa. In 1884, it had been agreed that southern Africa would be divided between the British, in Cape Province and Natal, and the Dutch Boer settlers in the Transvaal and the Orange Free State. But the British had overall control. And this is what created the problem, particularly

KEY FACTS

Governments, 1886–1914

after 1886 when gold was discovered in the Transvaal. The
British colonial secretary, Joseph Chamberlain, believed
that British supremacy in southern Africa was essential if
Britain was to remain an imperial power. And the gold was
an additional incentive. He, together with the British High
Commissioner in the Cape, put so much pressure on the
Boers that they had no option but to fight. This is what
the British wanted – a swift war and victory. What they
got was something a bit different.

The war was initially very popular and Prime Minister
Salisbury called a quick election in 1900. This 'khaki'
election resulted in a Conservative victory over the
Liberals, even though their majority was slightly reduced.
However,

- A significant number of British people were opposed to
  the war. Jeered at for being pro-Boer, they criticised the
  government on all possible occasions and questioned the
  morality of the war.
- Thousands of young men volunteered to fight. Roughly
  two volunteers in every three were rejected because they
  were medically unfit. People began wondering how it
  was that a supposedly prosperous country such as Britain
  could produce such weak and undernourished young
  people.
- The war lasted far longer and cost a great deal more than
  anyone anticipated. The British public was not expecting
  its soldiers to encounter such resistance and criticised the
  government for what seemed like incompetence.
- It took a supposedly well equipped and highly trained
  fighting force, the British army, three years to defeat an
  inexperienced group of badly equipped farmers. This led
  to despair at home and embarrassment and ridicule
  abroad.
- In order to break Boer resistance, the British army
  interned civilians in concentration camps where dreadful
  conditions led to the spread of fatal diseases. This led to
  further disquiet in Britain. Campbell-Bannerman
  described the army's methods as 'barbaric' and Lloyd
  George declared 'we are killing babies now'.

Wars are often catalysts for change. Old assumptions are

challenged and new approaches and ways of doing things are sought. Certainly, this war enabled the Liberal Party to regroup and refocus its political thinking and objectives. It caused, too, disquiet among the public about the Conservative Party's competency to govern in the interests of the people.

Was the 1902 Education Act responsible?

The Liberal Party had, traditionally, gained a lot of support from **non-conformists**. This was largely because of the importance liberalism placed on the freedom of individuals to think and believe as they wished. Towards the end of the nineteenth century there is evidence that this support was dwindling as the Conservative Party became an increasingly attractive alternative. However, after 1902, non-conformist support swung firmly back behind the Liberal Party. Why did this happen?

The 1870 Education Act (see page 3) set up board schools where there were no voluntary, church-run schools. These board schools were almost always in towns and they began to provide better elementary education than the voluntary church schools. The 1902 Education Act tried to even matters out:

- Voluntary schools run by the Church of England were to be funded from the **rates**.
- School boards were to be abolished. In future, elementary schools were to be run by local council education committees and paid for from the rates.

Non-conformists were furious. Their rates were going to help pay for Church of England and Roman Catholic schools. Non-conformists had always objected to what they saw as unfair privileges being enjoyed by the Church of England, and they saw this as just one more unacceptable privilege. They launched a fierce campaign against the Act. Because this campaign was supported by the Liberal Party, thousands of non-conformists renewed their support for the party, thus further weakening the Conservatives.

Was tariff reform responsible?

British manufacturers were becoming extremely concerned at a range of developments that were threatening to reduce their profits and even put them out of business altogether.

- Plant and machinery that had given Britain the lead in industrial processes were becoming outdated and lack of investment meant they were not replaced.
- Iron and steel production in the USA and Germany had overtaken that in Britain.
- Many of Britain's competitors had begun to place high tariffs (taxes) on imports from Britain and this was making it increasingly difficult to sell British goods abroad.

How was the situation to be resolved? **Free trade** had been a cornerstone of Conservative policy since the middle of the nineteenth century. Furthermore, to most British people, free trade meant prosperity and cheap food. To abandon free trade in favour of **protection** would be a risky policy for the Conservatives to adopt.

Joseph Chamberlain, the Secretary of State for the colonies, came up with a cunning plan. He proposed that the British government should put tariffs on all goods coming in to Britain, but that imports from the British empire should be subject to lower tariffs or no tariffs at all. He argued that in this way:

- British industry would be protected from foreign competition
- the British government would have money to spend on social reforms
- British links with the empire would be strengthened.

Chamberlain put forward these ideas in a public speech he made in Birmingham on 15 May 1903. The effect on the Conservative Party was explosive.

- The Conservative Party split between those who supported him and those who clung to the traditional ideas of free trade.

- Some Conservative MPs, like the young Winston Churchill, defected to the Liberals.
- Joseph Chamberlain resigned from the government to campaign full-time for **imperial preference**.

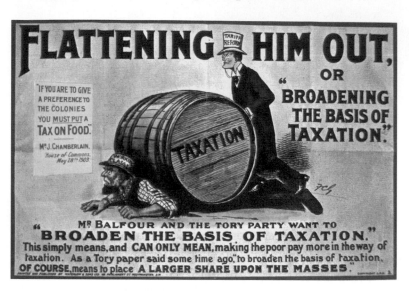

FLATTENING HIM OUT, OR **BROADENING THE BASIS OF TAXATION.**

"IF YOU ARE TO GIVE A PREFERENCE TO THE COLONIES YOU MUST PUT A TAX ON FOOD."

Mr J. CHAMBERLAIN, House of Commons, May 28th 1903.

" Mr BALFOUR AND THE TORY PARTY WANT TO **BROADEN THE BASIS OF TAXATION."** This simply means, and CAN ONLY MEAN, making the poor pay more in the way of taxation. As a Tory paper said some time ago, to broaden the basis of taxation, OF COURSE, means to place A LARGER SHARE UPON THE MASSES."

Liberal Party election poster of 1906

The Conservative government under Arthur Balfour adopted tariff reform as its official programme. Fierce debates on 'free trade v. protection' followed in the press and in Parliament. The Liberal Party was able to present itself as the defender of cheap food for the people.

Was Arthur Balfour responsible?

It seemed to many people that the Conservative government's troubles only really began when Arthur Balfour took over as prime minister when his uncle, Lord Salisbury, retired in July 1902. Was Balfour, quite simply, not up to the job?

- It was well known that Salisbury had serious doubts about the sense of promoting the Education Act of 1902 when so many non-conformists were firmly opposed to it. Nevertheless, Balfour steered the bill through Parliament and was so closely associated with it that it is often referred to as the 'Balfour Act'. Salisbury scented political danger; Balfour quite clearly did not.
- Balfour realised the electoral danger of Chamberlain's tariff reform proposals and wrote to Chamberlain pointing this out. Balfour was Prime Minister when the

KEY EVENTS

The Taff Vale case The Taff Vale Railway Company in South Wales refused to give its employees a pay rise. The company refused to recognise the right of its workers' union, the Amalgamated Society of Railway Servants, to negotiate with it and so the union called a strike. The company used 'black-leg' labour to break the strike and the dispute ended in defeat for the union. The company then sued the union for loss of income while its employees were on strike. In 1902 the case went to the House of Lords, who decided in favour of the Taff Vale Railway Company. The union was ordered to pay £23,000 in compensation. This meant that the right to strike was severely undermined because unions were liable to pay employers unlimited damages for revenue lost during a strike.

Lib–Lab pact of 1903 An agreement between the Liberal Party and the **Labour Representation Committee** (LRC) to defeat the Conservatives in the general election of 1906. They agreed that that no Liberal candidate would stand if the LRC candidate had a better chance of getting elected. In return, the LRC agreed to restrict the number of candidates standing elsewhere. In effect, the LRC was guaranteed Liberal votes to defeat Conservative candidates.

Conservative government adopted tariff reform as government policy. If he really had understood that this meant electoral disaster for his party, he should have acted more decisively in distancing himself and his party from Joseph Chamberlain and his ideas about imperial preference.

- Balfour's actions over Chinese slavery and the **Taff Vale** judgement seemed to reveal his lack of sympathy with working-class people and alienated their support.
  - Balfour's government allowed large numbers of Chinese labourers to work in South African gold and diamond mines in appalling conditions for very low wages. The British public were appalled. They were appalled on humanitarian grounds, and also feared that the government might, in hard times, import cheap foreign labour and undercut their wages. Balfour was opposed to the 'Chinese slavery' scheme but did nothing to stop it.
  - Judgement in the Taff Vale case meant that the rights of trade unions were severely restricted. The government's refusal to do anything to help trade unions after this judgement reinforced trade unions' belief that the government was fundamentally opposed to them. Trade unionists increasingly turned to the Liberals and the **Lib–Lab pact** of 1903 was made possible.

THE GENERAL ELECTION OF 1906

The Liberal Party swept to power in 1906, with 399 seats to the Conservative Party's 156 (see table on page 11). They were helped by:

- the failings of the Conservatives in the late 1890s and early 1900s that led to massive defections of voters who had previously voted Conservative
- the Liberal Party's ability to mobilise previously untapped support: turnout rose by 8 per cent over that in the 1900 election and was the highest since 1885
- the existence of Labour candidates in industrial constituencies where no Liberal candidate was standing

- the abstention of many Conservative voters who could not bring themselves to vote Liberal and who could not support Arthur Balfour.

It was very clear to the electors what the Liberal Party was against. It was against tariff reform and Chinese slavery, the 1902 Education Act and high public expenditure. But in 1906 it was far from clear what the Liberal Party stood for.

SUMMARY QUESTIONS

1 What contribution did
   (a) Joseph Chamberlain and
   (b) Arthur Balfour make to the defeat of the Conservatives in 1906?

2 Look carefully at the 1906 Liberal Party election poster on page 16.
   (a) How is it trying to persuade people to vote Liberal?
   (b) To which section of the electorate is it appealing?

3 Why did the Liberal Party have such a landslide victory in the general election of 1906?

KEY ORGANISATION

The Labour Representation Committee This was formed after a conference of socialists, ILP members and trade unionists was held in London in February 1900. Its aim was to establish a Labour group in Parliament to promote the direct interests of working people. In the general election of 1900, the LRC won two seats in Parliament. The 1903 pact with the Liberals led to success in the 1906 election, with LRC candidates winning 29 seats out of the 50 they contested. The LRC was renamed the Labour Party.

CHAPTER 2

The needs of the people: welfare and social reforms, 1906–14

The newly elected Liberal government embarked on a series of wide-ranging welfare reforms that were designed to lift the most vulnerable members of society – the sick and infirm, children and the elderly – out of poverty. These reforms were to change radically the ways in which governments dealt with poverty.

DID THE ELECTORATE EXPECT WELFARE REFORMS?

In the eight years before the First World War, the Liberal governments under first Henry Campbell-Bannerman and then Herbert Asquith embarked upon a sweeping programme of social and economic reform. The Liberal Party's election campaign had been largely negative, attacking the Conservatives' record but giving few clues as to what it would do if elected.

The extract below is part of a speech made by Asquith in Cambridge in 1904. He was to become Chancellor of the Exchequer under Campbell-Bannerman, and took over from him as Prime Minister in 1908 when ill-health forced Campbell-Bannerman from office.

> *The most serious burden upon the industry of Great Britain is the enormous and progressive increase in what the state is taking by taxation and by borrowing out of the pockets of the people of this country. If a Liberal government came into power, the first duty they set themselves would be a reduction in the country's expenditures.*

In his election address, Campbell-Bannerman didn't give much away, either:

Should we be confirmed in office, it will be our duty, whilst holding fast to the time-honoured principles of Liberalism – the principles of peace, economy, self-government and civil and religious liberty – and whilst resisting with all our strength the attack upon free trade, to repair, as far as lies in our power, the mischief wrought in recent years and, by a course of strenuous legislation and administration to secure those social and economic reforms which have been too long delayed.

WHAT REFORMS DID CAMPBELL-BANNERMAN'S GOVERNMENT CARRY OUT?

Henry Campbell-Bannerman began slowly. He was by nature cautious and had a front bench that was enthusiastic but largely untried in office. Moreover, although the Liberals dominated the Commons, the House of Lords had a built-in Conservative majority. Any legislation passed by the Commons had to gain the approval of the Lords before it could become law, and this was not necessarily going to be easy.

Lord Lansdowne (Conservative leader in the Lords) and Arthur Balfour (Conservative leader in the Commons) worked together to ensure that the only legislation that got through the Lords was that which was in the interests of the country, not the Liberal Party. This meant, for example, that an Education Bill that would have brought non-conformists firmly into the Liberal fold was thrown out. But legislation that directly helped the poorer and more vulnerable members of society did get onto the statute book.

Not all of the apparently progressive legislation listed on page 21 was introduced on the initiative of the government.

- The Liberal government was more or less forced into legislation to provide free meals for needy children as a result of the introduction of a private member's bill by the Labour MP William Wilson. Anxious not to be seen as less radical than the new Labour Party, the government made the bill its own.

The **1906 Trades Dispute Act** protected unions' right to strike and allowed peaceful picketing. In effect, this reversed the Taff Vale judgement (see page 17)

The **1906 Workers' Compensation Act** extended compensation paid for injuries at work to 6 million more workers. It included specific diseases and shortened the time gap between claim and payment.

The **1906 Merchant Shipping Act** improved working conditions for seamen.

The **1906 Education (Provision of Meals) Act** allowed local authorities to use public money to provide free meals for children of needy parents. Parents taking advantage of these meals for their children were not classified as **paupers**.

The **1907 Education (Administrative Procedures) Act** set up a school medical service, run by local authorities.

The **1908 Children and Young Persons' Act** brought together several older Acts and furthered their provisions:

- Children were made 'protected persons' which meant that their parents could be prosecuted for neglect or cruelty.

- Poor Law authorities were made responsible for visiting and supervising children who had suffered cruelty or neglect.

- Nursing homes and private children's homes were to be registered and inspected.

- Publicans were forbidden to let children under 14 years old into public houses.

- Shopkeepers were forbidden to sell cigarettes to children under 14 years old.

- Juvenile courts and remand homes were set up to separate children from adult offenders.

- Sir Robert Morant, the permanent secretary at the Board of Education (and therefore a civil servant) was determined to see medical provision introduced into the nation's schools. He managed to slip the relevant clauses into a complicated and technical piece of legislation and few MPs noticed or understood what he had done. Once the bill became law, Morant issued directives and circulars to local authorities, regulating the service and authorising them to provide treatment as well as inspection.

This first wave of reforming legislation was, however, significant for more than the actual help that was given to the needy and vulnerable. It showed quite clearly that the state was prepared to intervene in people's lives far more than it had in the past.

Campbell-Bannerman resigned because of ill-health in April 1908, and, with his resignation, the reforming zeal of the Liberal government moved up a gear.

DID ASQUITH'S GOVERNMENT PUSH BACK THE FRONTIERS OF REFORM?

The prime movers of reform in Asquith's government were the Chancellor of the Exchequer, David Lloyd George, and the President of the Board of Trade, Winston Churchill. Asquith and the rest of the Cabinet approved of their proposals and, in this sense, they can be said to be government initiatives. On the other hand, there is ample

Lloyd George and Winston Churchill in 1910

KEY LEGISLATION

Poor Law This was a series of laws, passed by Parliament in Elizabethan times, to provide help for people who were destitute. Before 1834 this help was based on the parish and was usually given in the form of money or goods to people in their own homes. This was called 'outdoor' relief. Different systems of poor relief grew up until, in 1834, the Poor Law Amendment Act tried to impose one national system. Any person needing relief was supposed to get help only in a workhouse, where the regime was harsh. In practice, outdoor relief continued in various forms and was the most common form of relief throughout the nineteenth century. Even so, the shadow of the workhouse affected the poor to such an extent that it was sometimes difficult to persuade them to accept new and different forms of help.

KEY TERMS

Deserving and undeserving poor Traditionally, the poor were divided into 'deserving' and 'undeserving'. The 'deserving' poor were widows and orphans, the sick and the old and were deemed to have become poor through no fault of their own. The 'undeserving' poor were the able-bodied poor who, it was believed, could find work for themselves or better work that would support themselves and their families. In a humanitarian state, help had to be given to save them from destitution.

evidence that many of their proposals were fiercely opposed by some members of the Cabinet – and that Churchill and Lloyd George were virtually the only members of the government who proposed any kind of reform.

The 1909 Old Age Pensions Act was promised in the 1908 budget and implemented in 1909. Pensions were paid to men and women over the age of 70 on a sliding scale according to the rest of their income. But there were conditions. To quality for a pension, men and women had to be British citizens who had been resident in Britain for 20 years. And they had to be of good character: pensions weren't paid to people who had been in prison during the previous ten years; who continually failed to find work; who had claimed poor relief in the past two years; or who were drunkards.

But was this in fact a break with the past?

- The number of people claiming pensions was around 600,000 – roughly the same as the elderly claiming poor relief before the Pensions Act.
- The payments were roughly the same, too. The usual weekly outdoor relief payment was 5 shillings per person – the same as a full pension for a single person.
- The idea of the **deserving and the undeserving poor** was still there.

Just how revolutionary, then, was the provision of old age pensions?

- Pensions were paid as a right, not at the discretion of a Poor Law officer.
- Pensions were paid at local post offices, so divorcing them even more from the **Poor Law**.
- Pensions were funded from national taxation, not from local poor rates.

Part 1 of the 1911 National Insurance Act was an attempt to provide help for the poor when ill-health struck the main breadwinner, while at the same time not harming vested interests like insurance companies and doctors who might lose income with a state insurance programme.

Employees, employers and the state all contributed and health cover was provided to workers in certain selected industries.

This was probably the most unpopular of all the Liberal government's welfare reforms:

- Most workers resented paying 4d from their wages.
- Payments were at a flat rate, and so they hit the poorest workers the hardest.
- Many workers regarded National Insurance payments as nothing more than a pay cut, arguing that it was a waste of money to insure against illnesses they might never have.

However, this was arguably the most important of all the Liberal government's welfare reforms. By 1913, 13 million workers were insured in the scheme and a very important safety net had been established.

The 1909 Labour Exchanges Act set up a series of nationally organised but regionally operated labour exchanges that were intended to help the unemployed find work. Jobs were advertised at one central point, saving workers from tramping round various workplaces.

Labour exchanges were an enormous success. But the exchanges themselves were only part of the story. Only by 'signing on' at a labour exchange was it known that a person was unemployed. Insurance against unemployment, therefore, was to form a further plank in the raft of provision for those who could not work, and Churchill had to wait to implement this and make the provision complete until Lloyd George had finalised his work on national health insurance.

Part 2 of the 1911 National Insurance Act provided workers with insurance against unemployment.

- Employers, employees and the government contributed in equal measure to the scheme.
- Workers could claim benefit for up to fifteen weeks in any one year, unless unemployment was the result of a person being sacked for misconduct.

The Act first applied to a group of trades where the pay was reasonably high but the work was prone to seasonal unemployment (ship building, for example). Insurance was compulsory, and 2.25 million men were insured by the end of 1912. Because of high employment in these trades and industries immediately before the First World War, it is impossible to evaluate its success. However, the Act is important for what it represented. Together with pensions and health insurance, it established the principle that providing relief for the poor and vulnerable was a national, not local responsibility.

HOW WERE THE REFORMS TO BE PAID FOR?

Clearly the Liberal reforms were expensive and, equally clearly, they were not self-funding. They were going to cost around £16 million and, initially, this had to be raised in the budget of 1909. This came at a time when additional money had to be found to fund the naval shipbuilding programme, intended to keep the Royal Navy more powerful than the German navy. All eyes were on the budget of 1909. Could Lloyd George, the Chancellor of the Exchequer, raise all this additional revenue and persuade Parliament to agree with him?

David Lloyd George, quite simply, taxed the rich and better off in order to fund help for the needy and vulnerable. He:

- increased taxes on tobacco by a quarter and on spirits by a third
- introduced a new tax on cars according to horsepower
- put a 3d per gallon tax on petrol
- raised income tax on a sliding scale, so that those with incomes of under £3000 a year paid 9d for every pound they earned; those with incomes over £3000 a year paid 1s 2d for every pound they earned; people with incomes over £5000 paid an additional super-tax of 6d in the pound
- increased death duties (now called inheritance tax) on estates worth more than £5000
- introduced a new tax on profits gained from selling land.

THE PHILANTHROPIC HIGHWAYMAN.

Mr. Lloyd-George. "*I'LL* MAKE 'EM PITY THE AGED POOR!"

This 'People's Budget' easily got through the House of Commons. But it was a different matter when it came to the House of Lords. Traditionally, the House of Lords never opposed a revenue measure. However, the Conservatives had an in-built majority in the Lords and many of them were large landowners. This budget would hit them and their class hard. So they threw it out.

This precipitated an enormous political crisis: the unelected Lords were defying the will of the elected Commons. The government had been denied the money it needed to govern as it thought fit. Asquith had no choice but to ask the King to dissolve Parliament and call a general election.

SUMMARY QUESTIONS

1 Look back at the reforms introduced by the Liberal governments. Who were they designed to help? Was there still an underclass they didn't reach?

2 Study the cartoon 'The Philanthropic Highwayman'. Would you agree with the message the cartoonist was trying to get across to readers of *Punch*?

3 How far did the Liberal reforms make a break with the past?

CHAPTER 3

Constitutional conflict: struggles with the Lords

The 'Peoples' Budget' of 1909 precipitated a huge constitutional crisis. The House of Lords had never before rejected a revenue bill, regarding it as the business of the Commons to raise money in order to run the country. The real issue therefore became one of who governed Britain – the unelected Lords or the elected Commons.

HAD THE LORDS REJECTED BILLS BEFORE 1909?

The constitutional position was quite clear. For a bill to become law, it had to have the approval of the House of Commons, the House of Lords and the monarch. No monarch had refused consent to a parliamentary bill since 1708 and Edward VII certainly wasn't going to refuse the proposals in the 1909 budget, as approved by the Commons. But it was a different matter in the Lords. With their inbuilt Conservative majority, the Lords had less qualms about rejecting Liberal legislation. They had, after all, done it before:

- In 1893, the Lords rejected the Liberal Party's **Home Rule** proposals master-minded by Gladstone.
- The Liberals' Education Bill of 1906, which would have reduced Anglican influence, was voted out by the Lords.
- The new Licensing Bill, passed by the Commons in 1908, was vetoed by the Lords because of pressure from the brewers – rich and highly influential men.
- Proposals to end plural voting, that would have affected Conservative-held constituencies more than Liberal ones, were also rejected.

So why didn't these issues result in a crisis? Liberal governments were, in the main, anxious to get what reforms they could without confronting the unelected Lords, and so they accepted rejections of what were, to

KEY IDEA

Home Rule The belief that the people of the island of Ireland should rule themselves and be independent of mainland Britain.

them, relatively minor issues. But reform of the Lords had been one of Gladstone's unachieved aims; and there is evidence that Campbell-Bannerman was preparing for a show-down with the Lords just before his death. Lloyd George certainly delivered one.

WHY WAS THE PEOPLE'S BUDGET OF 1909 SO CONTROVERSIAL?

This budget was controversial from the start because it marked a completely new approach to taxation. In the past, taxation had been raised to pay for government expenditure on, for example, defence. Now, it was being used to redistribute wealth. Taxes were being targeted on the rich in order to fund state schemes to help the poorest members of society, and the Conservatives didn't like it. They argued that the budget was an unprecedented attack on property, and that this entitled them to ignore the long-standing convention that the Lords did not interfere with money bills.

Lord Lansdowne, in a speech to the House of Lords on 22 November 1909, urged the Lords to view the People's Budget in a new light:

> *Is this an ordinary budget? His Majesty's ministers have never ceased explaining that it is anything but an ordinary budget. Take the language of the Prime Minister a few weeks ago in the City. He spoke of the budget as having 'far reaching political and social results' – political and social, mind you, not financial. It is idle to talk of the bill as being an ordinary budget bill, for it is not.*

Did Lloyd George deliberately engineer a conflict with the Lords?

Lloyd George hated privilege of any kind, and landed privilege most of all. It was clear that he would relish a conflict with the Lords, but did he deliberately provoke one in the expectation that a constitutional crisis would break out? It seems unlikely for two main reasons:

• both Asquith and Lloyd George gave priority to the

Liberal reform programme; any constitutional conflict would delay reforming legislation;
- by 1909, rank-and-file Liberals were beginning to become disillusioned by what they perceived as the limited nature of the reforms. Lloyd George and Asquith were looking for a way of kick-starting the reform programme and a massive injection of cash was necessary for this. They last thing they would have wanted was a protracted constitutional struggle.

WHY WAS THERE A CONSTITUTIONAL CRISIS?

In November 1909, the House of Lords rejected Lloyd George's Budget Bill. Why should this precipitate a constitutional crisis?

What was the real issue?

The real issue concerned who governed Britain. Was it the unelected House of Lords who regarded themselves as members of the natural governing classes? Or was it the elected majority in House of Commons who formed a government by the will of the people?

Why did the Liberal government confront the House of Lords?

The Liberal government could have simply accepted the budget's rejection and amended it so that it met with the approval of the Lords. There didn't automatically have to be a conflict. But to do this would have delayed and maybe even stopped the Liberal reforming programme in its tracks. There were issues of principle, too:

- The Commons had to control taxation in order to ensure that they had enough money to govern the country properly.
- The Liberal government had a massive majority in the Commons and therefore a mandate to continue its reforming programme and to raise the money for it.
- The Lords traditionally regarded themselves as the 'guardians of the constitution'. By rejecting the 1909 budget, they were acting in a blatantly partisan way to

support the interests of the Conservative Party and not in any way to protect the constitution.

Why did Conservative peers oppose the People's Budget?

It is easy to look on the reasons for peers' rejection of the budget as one of blatant self-interest. For some it was but for many, however, it was the culmination of years of frustration. Most peers feared for the future.

- The late-nineteenth-century agricultural depression resulted in a fall of rents and land prices, and consequently income for the landowning peers.
- Electoral reforms made it difficult for landowners to influence the way their employees voted.
- Local government reforms had shifted the centre of power from the hereditary aristocracy and gentry to those who were elected to institutions such as local councils, school boards and boards of guardians.
- Recent by-election successes led the Lords to believe that, if they found an issue on which they could challenge the Commons, the Conservatives stood a good chance of being successful in any resultant general election.
- There was a widespread belief that the People's Budget, if implemented, would pave the way for the financing of further reforms by taxing the rich.

Lloyd George claimed the budget was a declaration of war on poverty; the House of Lords saw it as a declaration of war on property.

Stepping-stones through the crisis

The rejection of the People's Budget led automatically to a general election because, without funds, a government cannot govern. Asquith and Lloyd George made the election a 'one issue' election: a straightforward contest between peers and people. David Lloyd George certainly gave his emotive rhetoric full rein. In a speech to the Commons in 1910 he declared:

> *They are forcing a revolution and they will get it. The Lords may decree a revolution but the people will direct it. If they*

"THE PEER GLASS"

Picture of a Peer consulting his constituents. Though it may be all very well for him to represent no one but himself, where do YOU come in?

begin, issues will be raised that they little dream of. Questions will be asked which are now whispered in humble voices and answers will be demanded then with full authority. The question will be asked whether five hundred men, ordinary men chosen accidentally from the unemployed, should override the judgement – the deliberate judgement – of millions of people who are engaged in the industry which makes the wealth of the country. That is one question. Another will be: Who made ten thousand people owners of the soil, and the rest of us trespassers in the land of our birth? Who is it who is responsible for the scheme of things whereby one man is engaged through life in grinding labour to win a bare and precarious subsistence for himself, and when, at the end of his days, he claims at the hands of the community he served a poor pension of eight pence a day, he can only get it through a revolution, and another man who does not toil receives every hour of the day, every hour of the night, whilst he slumbers, more than his poor neighbour receives in a whole year of toil?

He mocked the Lords for being not 'the watchdog of the constitution' but 'Mr Balfour's poodle'.

But what actually happened?

- A general election was held in **January 1910**. The Conservatives, desperate to remove proposals for taxes on land, suggested tariff reform as an alternative way of raising revenue. It didn't do them much good.
- The Liberals were returned in roughly equal numbers to the Conservatives. This was not the result the Liberals had wanted. Asquith and the Liberals were kept in office by 40 Labour Party MPs and 82 Irish Nationalists, who thought their own interests were best served by allying with the Liberals rather than the Conservatives. A high price was demanded for this support: Labour demanded favourable trade union legislation; and the Irish demanded a Home Rule bill.
- Reluctantly, the Lords passed the People's Budget in **April 1910**. The focus of the Liberals now shifted to constitutional reform.
- King Edward VII insisted that, before Asquith moved against the Lords, a second general election had to be held so that the will of the people on this particular issue could be determined. But, in **May 1910**, the king died.
- A constitutional conference failed to find a way out of the political deadlock. Asquith asked for, and got from the new king, George V, a dissolution of Parliament and a general election. This general election was, again, a single-issue one, as Asquith made clear in an election speech on 10 December 1910:

> *For what is our actual Second Chamber? It is a body which has no pretensions or qualifications to be the organ or interpreter of the popular will. It is a body in which one party of state is in possession of an overwhelming majority. It is a body which, as experience shows, in temper and in action, is frankly and nakedly partisan. It is a body which does not attempt to exercise any kind of effective control over the legislation in the Commons when its own party is in a majority there. It is a body which, when the conditions are reversed, however clear an emphatic the verdict of the country may have been, sets itself to work to mutilate and to obstruct*

democratic legislation and even, in these last days, to usurp the control of the democratic finance. We are not proposing the abolition of the House of Lords or setting up a single Chamber, but we do ask the electors to say that the House of Lords shall be confined to the proper functions of a Second Chamber. The absolute veto which it at present possesses must go. The people in future when they elect a new House of Commons must be able to feel, what they cannot feel now, that they are sending to Westminster men who will have the power not merely of proposing and debating, but of making laws. The will of the people, as expressed by their elected representatives, must within the limits of a single Parliament, be made effective.

- The outcome of the general election of **December 1910** was much the same as the one held earlier in the year.

	Conservative	Liberal	Labour	Irish Nationalist
January	273	275	40	82
December	272	272	42	84

General election results, 1910

The Parliament bill 1911

The return of the Liberals guaranteed action against the Lords, although the Conservatives claimed that the Liberals had no clear mandate from the people for doing any such thing. While a second Parliament bill, removing the Lords veto, made its way through the Commons, Lord Lansdowne, the Conservative leader in the Lords, desperately put forward new proposals to reconstitute and strengthen what he regarded as 'his' Chamber. When the bill finally arrived in the Lords, they changed it completely. However, their opposition wavered when Landsdowne and Balfour discovered that the new king, George V, was reluctantly prepared to create up to 500 Liberal peers if the Lords defied the Commons a second time. Not only would the Parliament bill become law, but there would be a built-in Liberal majority in the Lords and all sorts of uncomfortably progressive reforms would get on to the statute books. The Lords split into 'hedgers' who were prepared to consider compromise and surrender, and 'ditchers' who were prepared to fight to the last ditch.

The Parliament Act 1911

The power of the Lords was significantly reduced:

- The Lords could delay a bill by no more than two years.
- Any bill sent from the Commons in three consecutive sessions would automatically become law despite being rejected by the Lords.

There were other important provisions:

- MPs were to receive a salary
- the life of parliaments was reduced from seven to five years.

When the crucial vote came, abstentions and the decision of 37 Conservative peers to vote for the bill resulted in a majority of seventeen in its favour. The Lords had lost the battle, but not necessarily the war.

What were the immediate outcomes of the constitutional crisis?

- The built-in Conservative majority in the Lords remained.
- The Lords could now only delay legislation important to the Commons, such as an Irish Home Rule bill.
- Now that MPs were paid, the Labour Party could field more candidates in by-elections and general elections.
- Arthur Balfour lost the leadership of the Conservative Party and was replaced by Andrew Bonar Law.
- The Liberals were able to press ahead with their legislative programme of reform.

SUMMARY QUESTIONS

1 Why did the People's Budget precipitate a constitutional crisis?

2 Read Asquith's speech on pages 33–34. He made the speech just before the general election in December 1910. What does the speech reveal about
(a) what he wants and
(b) why he wants it?

3 The 'Peer's Glass' poster was produced for the government during the constitutional crisis.

(a) What is the message of the poster?

Look back at the cartoon 'The Philanthropic Highwayman' on page 26.

(b) What is the message of the cartoon?
(c) Do you think the poster or the cartoon is better at getting its message across to the public?

4 To what extent did the constitutional crisis end in triumph for the Liberals?

CHAPTER 4

New thinking

Before we begin looking at new and different challenges to the Liberal government, we need to stand back and ask where the ideas that underpinned the Liberal reforms actually came from. Why did Lloyd George and Churchill begin their intensive concerns for the needy and vulnerable? Why did Liberal thinking about the role of the state change?

WHAT WAS THE IMPACT OF INVESTIGATIONS AND SURVEYS?

In the latter years of the nineteenth century, there had been a growing interest in the poor, poverty and the cost of supporting paupers. Investigative journalists, like Henry Mayhew (1812–87) who wrote a series of articles for the *Morning Chronicle*, alerted the reading public to the plight of the poor. There were many local surveys of the needs of the poor, and Christian groups like the Salvation Army began bringing practical help to the needy and outcast. By the early years of the twentieth century, more quantitative, scientific surveys were being carried out.

Charles Booth (1840–1916) was responsible for the first scientific estimates of poverty and the development of survey methods in social investigation. A wealthy shipowner who moved his offices to London, he refused to accept official statistics that about 25 per cent of the working population were living in poverty. He conducted his own investigations, between 1886 and 1903, into the life and labour of London's poor, and published his findings in seventeen volumes. While these focused mainly on poverty, some of the volumes were also about industry, employment and religion. He found, on the basis of information supplied by 4000 people, that the proportion of Londoners living in poverty was closer to 30.7 per cent than 25 per cent. These people lived below the **poverty line**. They lacked the money to buy reasonable food,

KEY CONCEPT

Poverty line This is the level below which families have insufficient money to maintain a minimum acceptable standard of living. As the standard of living rises, so does the poverty line.

shelter and clothing. Booth went on to try to sort out the causes of poverty. He found that 85 per cent of those living in poverty were poor because of problems relating to employment: unemployment, short-time working or low pay.

Benjamin Seebohm Rowntree (1871–1954), who is usually referred to as Seebohm Rowntree, was the son of the chocolate magnate, Joseph Rowntree. He built on Charles Booth's work by investigating poverty in York, where the family business was based, hoping to give more precision to Booth's poverty line. Rowntree found that around 28 per cent of the population of York were living 'in obvious want and squalor'. He calculated that the minimum income required by a family of five simply to exist was 21s 8d. This was Rowntree's poverty line. To live below this poverty line was to live, Rowntree argued, in **primary poverty**. These families didn't stand a chance. To live just above this poverty line, where the necessities of life could be bought, but with nothing left over for extras or emergencies, was to live in **secondary poverty**. Rowntree began to uncover what he called a 'poverty cycle' where an individual slipped in and out of primary poverty.

Charles Booth's work *Life and Labour of the People in London* was started in 1886 and completed in 1903, and Seebohm Rowntree's *Poverty, a Study of Town Life* was published in 1901. Both studies had an impact on the thinking public, among whom we must include politicians.

The Royal Commission on the Poor Laws was set up by the Conservative government in 1905. It was to enquire into the workings of the poor laws and to advise the government on the best ways of relieving the poor. The commission

KEY TERMS

Primary poverty People living in primary poverty cannot obtain even the basic necessities of life (food, shelter and clothing) no matter how well they organise and manage their budgets. These families are living on the edge.

Secondary poverty People living in secondary poverty can obtain the basic necessities of life (food, shelter and clothing) provided there are no extra calls on their budget.

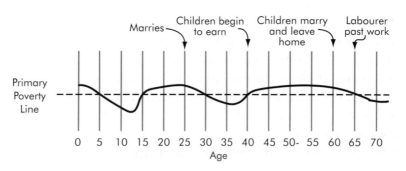

Rowntree's poverty line and poverty cycle

consisted of people with a wide range of appropriate
expertise: poor law guardians, members of charitable
organisations, religious and trade union leaders as well as
Charles Booth and Beatrice Webb. The commission made
thousands of visits and collected nearly 50 volumes of
evidence. But, when they came to write their final report
and make recommendations to the government, they
couldn't agree. So they wrote two reports.

The majority report said:

- The origins of poverty were basically moral.
- The poor law should remain the main way of delivering
  relief to the needy.
- Boards of Guardians had in the past allowed too much
  outdoor relief and this should be replaced by help given
  by public assistance committees, allowing the guardians
  to focus on help given in workhouses.
- There should be greater cooperation between charities
  and those administering the poor laws.

The minority report said:

- The origins of poverty were basically economic.
- A Ministry of Labour should be set up to introduce and
  oversee public works schemes; set up a chain of national
  labour exchanges to help the unemployed find jobs;
  organise a schedule of training schemes; set up detention
  colonies for those who were deliberately idle.
- The poor law should be broken up into: education
  committees to deal with child poverty; pension
  committees to deal with the problems of the elderly
  poor; and health committees to deal with the poor who
  were sick or infirm.

So, what was to be done? If a royal commission produces
two reports which are diametrically opposed a government
does not feel compelled to take notice of either set of
recommendations. In this case, the ranks of those who
supported 'no change' were strengthened by the majority
report, and so the actual recommendations of that report
tended to be overlooked. But, both reports from the Royal
Commission were, nevertheless, important. The Commission

had collected a vast amount of evidence and had succeeded in giving the problem of poverty a higher profile.

NATIONAL EFFICIENCY

In the early years of the twentieth century, there was much debate among socialists, Liberals and Conservatives on the subject of national efficiency. There was concern that the British economy and workforce were not operating at peak efficiency and that Britain would, inevitably, fall behind as a world power. These fears had been heightened by:

- revelations about poverty, disease and general physical weakness among working-class people, made by investigators such as Booth and Rowntree
- revelations about the physical state of those volunteering to fight in the Boer War
- the length of time it took supposedly crack troops in the British army to defeat an army of ill-equipped Boer farmers
- the speed with which American and German industry was overtaking British industry in production levels
- the growth of highly mobile European armies and the shipbuilding programmes of France, Russia and Germany that emphasised the vulnerability of Britain.

All this gave rise to a great deal of anxiety, debate and the publication of many papers and articles. Criticisms tended to focus on:

- the system of parliamentary government, where it was believed that government was increasingly run by amateurs, who were incompetent in the fields of administration and incapable of generating social policy, and who spent their time in party political squabbles
- the perceived amateurism of army officers and the inadequate training of their men
- the authority of the Treasury, where conservative thinking kept a tight rein on the purse strings, where support for innovation and social reconstruction should have been given.

Advocates of national efficiency supported state intervention in the field of welfare, and improvements in secondary education, particularly on the scientific and technical sides. They wanted more experts and businessmen involved in government, a reduction of parliamentary interference, a rationalisation and streamlining of local government and military training for all men. This sort of programme attracted a wide range of support, from **Fabian** socialists, progressive Liberals and liberal-minded Conservatives.

NEW LIBERALISM

By 1906, a new type of Liberalism seemed to be emerging, and it was this that provided the inspiration for the reforms that were made in the period 1906–14. Where had these ideas come from?

What was New Liberalism in theory?

In the final two decades of the nineteenth century, when in opposition, the Liberal Party had rethought a lot of its basic principles and strategies. This 'New Liberalism' had been greatly influenced by the philosopher **T. H. Green** and the writer J. A. Hobson. Under their guidance, a new approach was drawn up by radical Liberals and presented to the party as the way forward. The New Liberals argued that, in the past, Liberals had been too concerned with individual liberty. This had led them to ignore the needs of those who lived and worked in such appalling conditions that they were denied the liberties that the Liberal Party were striving so earnestly to promote. New Liberals argued that the state had to intervene to help the most vulnerable in society because to live in poverty, hardship and uncertainty meant they were denied individual liberty.

What was New Liberalism in practice?

The basis of New Liberalism was a change in attitude towards the state and how the state should operate in relation to its citizens. The table shows how the basic thinking of 'New Liberals' differed from that of 'Old Liberals'.

KEY GROUP

The Fabians Founded in 1894, the Fabians were a group of middle-class intellectuals who agreed, by and large, with Marx's analysis of the evils of the capitalist system, but they did not agree that socialism could come about only by revolution. They wanted to reshape society gradually, and 'according to the highest moral principles'. In the early days, George Bernard Shaw and Sidney and Beatrice Webb were its most prominent members, writing brilliant tracts that helped develop Labour Party policies. Still in existence, it remains an influential left-wing 'think tank'.

KEY PERSON

T. H. Green (1836-82)
Thomas Hill Green was a philosopher. He believed that people of different social classes could be united through the concept of 'citizenship.' He believed that the idea that we are all citizens of one country, with rights and responsibilities, would need to be backed by social welfare reforms funded by the state.

Differences between New and Old Liberalism

	'Old' Liberalism	'New' Liberalism
The role of the state	The state should interfere as little as possible in the workings of market forces.	There are circumstances in which the state should intervene.
Welfare provision	The state should not intervene because people would have no incentive to help themselves.	The state should help the poorest members of society and in so doing would provide them with liberty.
Taxes	Taxes should be as low as possible to enable people to spend their money as they wish.	Taxes should be raised to pay for welfare schemes designed to help vulnerable members of society.

However, there wasn't an enormous split between Old and New Liberals, and the New Liberals were themselves anxious to distance themselves from socialists in order to maintain their appeal to the wider Liberal electorate. They emphasised points of continuity with the Old Liberals.

- Both groups focused on the importance of the individual and individual initiatives.
- Both preferred social services to be funded by voluntary contributions.
- Both distinguished between 'deserving' and 'undeserving' poor.
- Both wanted to provide hard-working and 'deserving' members of the working class with the opportunity to enjoy a middle-class standard of living.

Who were the New Liberals?

Support for New Liberalism in the country at large came mainly from the middle classes, from journalists and doctors, teachers, lawyers and writers. Many of them were in contact with socialist thinkers and supporters of the new **Independent Labour Party**. However, they were at pains to distance themselves from the far-left views about class conflict, and the calls from socialists for state ownership of industry and commerce.

About half of the Liberal MPs elected in 1906 supported New Liberalism. However, as you have seen, the Liberals had no welfare reform programme in mind when they swept to power in 1906. It is clear that David Lloyd George, who was President of the Board of Trade 1906–8 and Chancellor of the Exchequer 1908–15, was in sympathy with the ideas of the New Liberals. Together with Winston Churchill, who took over from Lloyd George at the Board of Trade, he worked out a complete programme of reform that was planned to regenerate the nation. It also stole the thunder from the new Labour Party by bringing state welfare to the working classes.

In October 1906, David Lloyd George made a speech in Cardiff in which he set out his thinking:

> I can tell the Liberals what will make this Independent Labour Party movement a great and sweeping force in this country – a force that will sweep away Liberalism amongst other things. If at the end of an average term of office it were found that a Liberal parliament had done nothing to cope seriously with the social condition of the people, to remove the national degradation of slums, and widespread poverty and destitution in a land glittering with wealth; that they had shrunk from attacking boldly the causes of this wretchedness; that they had not arrested the waste of our national resources in armaments, nor provided an honourable sustenance for deserving old age; that they had tamely allowed the House of Lords to extract all the virtue out of their bills; then would a real cry arise from the land for a new party, and many of us here in this room would join in that cry. But if a Liberal government tackled these issues, then the Independent Labour Party will call in vain upon the working men of Britain to desert Liberalism that is so gallantly fighting to rid the land of the wrongs that have oppressed those who labour in it.

Winston Churchill turned this rhetoric into more practical paths in a speech in the same month:

> It is through the agency of the Liberal Party alone that society will, in the course of time, slide forward almost painlessly on to a more even and equal foundation. This is the mission of

Keir Hardie (1856–1915)
Born into extreme poverty in Scotland, he worked in coal mines from the age of ten. He tried to organise the Lanarkshire and Ayrshire miners, and became secretary of the Scottish Miners' Federation in 1886. A year later, he was chairman of the Scottish Labour Party. In 1892, he was elected an independent Labour MP for South West Ham and the following year he founded the Independent Labour Party. He was instrumental in founding the Labour Representation Committee in 1900 and became chairman of the Parliamentary Labour Party in 1906. A pacifist, trade unionist and supporter of women's suffrage, he never held public office but did much to build the Labour Party into a credible alternative to the Conservatives as a party of government.

HEINEMANN ADVANCED HISTORY

the Liberal Party. Our cause is the cause of the left out millions.

I would like to see the Government embark on various adventurous experiments. We are all agreed that the state must concern itself with the care of the sick, of the aged and, above all, of the children. I do not want to limit the vigour of competition, but to mitigate the consequences of failure.

The Government will not hesitate to use its powers to establish universal standards of life and labour, and to raise these standards as increasing productive energy permits. We must not let ourselves be scared away from a plan just because some old women tell us that it is socialism.

SUMMARY QUESTIONS

1 How reliable were the findings of Booth and Rowntree about poverty?

2 How helpful do you find the concept of a 'poverty line'?

3 Why did some people become concerned with the whole idea of national efficiency? Do you think they were justified in their concern?

4 Was 'New Liberalism' anything more than a reaction to circumstances?

CHAPTER 5

Struggles for the suffrage

The activities of the militant **suffragettes** hit the headlines many times in the years before the First World War. But the demands for female **suffrage** were only part of the problem that surrounded the whole issue of who should have the right to vote. They were issues that shook and divided the Liberal government, weakened its moral standing and caused it severe political embarrassment. Suffrage issues divided Conservatives, too, and indeed there was never a clear divide across the established male political spectrum as to when, whether or how the suffrage should be extended.

WHAT MAIN ISSUES SURROUNDED THE SUFFRAGE QUESTION?

Traditionally, suffrage was less about the rights of individuals and more about the creation of effective, representative government. Those who could vote for this, so the argument went, were those who, by reason of their education, property, political knowledge and standing in society, could be trusted to exercise their vote in a responsible way. Women were automatically excluded. Men who spent their working lives in a daily struggle for existence could not develop these qualities. Neither could these qualities be demonstrated by those who depended on the state for their maintenance: men in receipt of poor relief could not vote. It followed that the interests of non-electors could be represented by community leaders. Thus, landowners could speak for their labourers, mill owners for their factory hands – and husbands for their wives. But as the nineteenth century came to an end and the twentieth began, this traditional view began to be eroded:

- By 1890 (see page 10), some women were fully involved in politics at a local level.

(see page 10)

KEY TERMS

Suffrage and **franchise**
The right to vote.

KEY GROUPS

Suffragists Those who used peaceful methods to persuade people that women should have the vote. The term usually refers to members of the National Union of Women's Suffrage Societies (NUWSS) formed in 1897 from several smaller women's suffrage societies and led by Millicent Fawcett.

Suffragettes A term made up by the *Daily Mail* to refer to members of the Women's Social and Political Union (WSPU), led by Emmeline and Christabel Pankhurst and given to militant activities to draw attention to women's right to vote.

- Both Conservative and Liberal parties formed women's branches. The Conservative Party founded the Primrose League in 1883; this was followed in 1887 by the Women's Liberal Foundation. Although many members of both organisations would have agreed with Mrs Gladstone that they were there 'to help our husbands', some women began to demand full political rights for themselves.

The boundaries between local and national politics were becoming blurred.

However, obstacles to women's enfranchisement still remained.

- There was no universal male suffrage at the beginning of the twentieth century, so the question of giving the vote to all women before it was given to all men was a non-starter.
- Once the majority of men were enfranchised after 1884, most of the remaining male non-voters did not support the cause of female suffrage but stood firm on their superior status as men.
- Political parties were much exercised by what the female vote would actually do. Would female voters tend to vote Liberal or Conservative? Or even Labour? Party officials were not going to recommend any extension of the franchise until it was reasonably clear where the women's vote would actually go and which party would benefit.
- The first priority for the Labour Party, insofar as the franchise was concerned, was the enfranchisement of all adult males. It was afraid that to support the extension of the franchise for selected groups of women would weaken the case for complete male suffrage.
- Many trade unions – especially the miners – were dominated by a masculine culture that made them uneasy about supporting votes for women.
- Not all women believed that women should be given the vote. In 1889 Mrs Humphrey Ward became president of the Anti-Suffrage League, declaring:

To men belong the struggle of debate and legislation in Parliament; the hard and exhausting labour implied in the *administration of the national resources and powers; the conduct of England's relations towards the external world; the working of the army and navy; all the heavy, laborious fundamental industries of the State, such of those of mines, metals and railways; the lead and supervision of English commerce, the management of our vast English finance, the service of the merchant fleet on which our food supply depends. In all these spheres, women's direct participation is made impossible either by the disabilities of sex*, or by strong formations of custom and habit resting ultimately on physical difference, against which it is useless to contend. Therefore it is not just to give to women direct power of deciding questions of Parliamentary policy, of war, of foreign or colonial affairs, of commerce and finance equal to that possessed by men.*

* women's menstrual cycle

HOW WAS THE CAMPAIGN FOR WOMEN'S SUFFRAGE ORGANISED?

The National Union of Women's Suffrage Societies (NUWSS)

In 1897 the NUWSS united suffrage groups from all over England under the presidency of **Millicent Fawcett**. Although it claimed to be non-political, many high-profile members were also members of the Women's Liberal Federation, which was sympathetic to the aims of the Liberal Party or had ready access through family or friends to decision-making members of the party.

In general, though, members of the NUWSS came from a wide social spectrum, although this tended to vary from region to region. The North of England Society for Women's Suffrage, affiliated to the NUWSS, was determined to broaden the class appeal of the campaign and several working-class women were involved at senior level. Some groups, like the Lancashire and Cheshire Women Textile and Other Workers Representation Committee, were founded specifically by and for working-class women. By the end of the nineteenth century, NUWSS branches were found throughout Britain; by 1910 the membership numbered around 21,500 with

KEY PERSON

Millicent Fawcett (1847–1929) Millicent Fawcett was born in Aldeburgh, Suffolk, the seventh of ten children. One of her sisters was Elizabeth Garrett Anderson, the second woman to qualify as a doctor in Britain. In 1867, she married the political economist and reformer, Henry Fawcett. His blindness meant she worked as his political secretary, introducing her to the world of politics. In 1868 she made her first public speech on women's suffrage. She was active in campaigning for university education for girls and founded Newnham College, Cambridge, in 1871. She became president of the National Union of Women's Suffrage Societies in 1897 and worked to obtain the vote for women by constitutional means and tried to strengthen ties between the NUWSS and the political parties. During the First World War she urged support for the war, but, unlike Mrs Pankhurst, continued to press the women's suffrage cause.

thousands more supporters and male 'associates' throughout the country.

Emmeline Pankhurst (1858–1928) Born in Manchester as the eldest of ten children, Emmeline's father was a well-off radical cotton manufacturer. In 1874, she married Richard Pankhurst, a left-wing lawyer. She followed him into the Fabian Society and the Independent Labour Party. She was elected a poor law guardian in 1893 and a school board member in 1900. Angered by the failure of the ILP to embrace the cause of women's suffrage, and irritated by what they perceived as the failure of the NUWSS to make sufficient progress in the cause, Emmeline and her daughter Christabel founded the Women's Social and Political Union in 1903. Moving to London in 1905, they adopted militant and increasingly illegal tactics, alienating many, but keeping the cause of women's suffrage in the public eye. In 1914, Emmeline abandoned militancy and worked on various army recruitment campaigns. After the war she lived briefly in Canada and then returned to England to stand unsuccessfully as a Conservative candidate for Whitechapel, London, in the 1926 election.

Women's Social and Political Union (WSPU)

In 1903, **Emmeline Pankhurst**, dissatisfied with what she saw as the failure of the NUWSS to deliver and the ambiguity of the Labour Party on the issue, set up the Women's Social and Political Union. Unlike the NUWSS, its structure was autocratic: what Mrs Pankhurst and her daughter **Christabel** (see page 49) said, went. Members, certainly in London where the WSPU eventually had its headquarters, did not take part in decision-making, although there is some evidence that provincial branches were more democratic. Because they controlled their publications, appointments and finances, it was difficult for ordinary members to oppose Emmeline and Christabel. It seems that the more the WSPU moved into dubious and even illegal activities, the more autocratic the Pankhursts became. Frequently criticised for being a predominantly middle-class organisation, the WSPU's roots lay in industrial Manchester where working-class women in the textile towns were recruited in greater numbers than joined the NUWSS. Initially welcoming male support, by 1913 the WSPU was unwilling to cooperate with men. It would not allow men to join the organisation and continually affirmed women's independence from men.

No matter what campaigning was done outside Parliament, the real battle was to win the hearts and minds of MPs because it was in Westminster that the fight for women's suffrage would be won. All the female suffrage bills before 1900 had been private members' bills. They didn't stand a chance unless the government of the day was prepared to give up government time to see them through all the proper stages. And, as no government had been prepared to do this, the bills had failed. The WSPU's core objective, therefore, was to put such pressure on a government that it brought in a women's suffrage bill.

In 1905, the Pankhursts moved to London and focused their attentions on the forthcoming general election. The Liberal landslide gave hope to those supporting women's suffrage because there was a large body of MPs who were

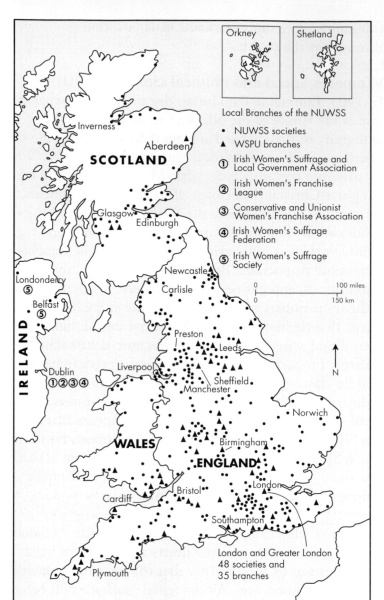

The spread of women's suffrage organisations throughout Britain by 1910

Local Branches of the NUWSS

• NUWSS societies
▲ WSPU branches
① Irish Women's Suffrage and Local Government Association
② Irish Women's Franchise League
③ Conservative and Unionist Women's Franchise Association
④ Irish Women's Suffrage Federation
⑤ Irish Women's Suffrage Society

London and Greater London
48 societies and
35 branches

sympathetic to the cause, among them David Lloyd George.

WHAT METHODS WERE USED IN THE SUFFRAGE CAMPAIGNS?

In the early days, those campaigning for the right of women to vote in general elections used, for most of the time, traditional middle-class methods of persuasion:

meetings and demonstrations, lobbying and letter writing. Later, the WSPU turned to more confrontational methods, but it still combined these with the more traditional approaches favoured by the NUWSS.

Meetings and conferences, held in places as far apart as Glasgow and Bristol, Norwich and Dublin, were used by both the NUWSS and WSPU to raise the profile of their campaigns, increase funds, disseminate propaganda and recruit new members. Additionally:

- Suffrage workers were provided to talk, by invitation, to smaller groups in their own homes or church and community halls and factory canteens.
- Suffrage supporters raised suffrage issues at conferences, such as those of the Trades Union Congress, and meetings organised by the main political parties.
- The WSPU broke new ground by addressing groups of women in the open air, from Trafalgar Square to factory gates and village greens.
- On 13 February 1907, to coincide with the opening of the new parliament, the WSPU held what it called the 'first women's parliament' in Caxton Hall, Westminster, across the road from the Houses of Parliament, as a protest against being excluded from the franchise.
- In 1908, Millicent Fawcett became the first woman to debate, and to debate on the question of women's suffrage, in the Oxford Union
- Generally, these were legal and well conducted, but in 1905 Christabel Pankhurst and **Annie Kenney** were arrested for heckling Winston Churchill at a Liberal Party election meeting in Manchester.

Marches and demonstrations were commonly used by the NUWSS and the WSPU. Not only did they bring 'the cause' visibly to the attention of people, but they engendered a sense of purpose and unity among the marchers.

- In February 1907, the NUWSS held a large open-air demonstration to coincide with the opening of the new parliament. More than 3000 women marched to Hyde

Park Corner in the pouring rain and the march was quickly nicknamed the 'Mud March'.

- In November 1910, 300 suffragettes tried to storm the lobby of the House of Commons. In the battle with police outside, many suffragettes were sexually and physically assaulted by the police, and all 135 sworn statements taken afterwards testified to this. The day was know as 'Black Friday' and many suffragettes were arrested, among them Emmeline and Christabel Pankhurst. They kept their cause in the public eye by going on hunger strike while in prison.
- In 1911, 40,000 demonstrators joined a London-based march to celebrate the new king, George V.
- A pilgrimage from Edinburgh to London in 1912 attracted thousands of supporters.
- In 1913, the WSPU turned the funeral of the suffragette Emily Wilding Davison, who threw herself under the king's horse during the Derby, into a political demonstration.

Propaganda was used by all suffrage groups and took many different forms. For example:

- The Artist's Suffrage League designed, printed and published a wide range of posters.
- Members of the Actresses' Franchise League wrote a large number of pro-suffrage plays, scenes and playlets that they performed in drawing rooms, village halls and theatres.
- Music and poetry, songs and limericks were composed and sung, whistled and declaimed whenever and wherever possible. Dame Ethel Smythe composed *The March of the Women* that became the WSPU's marching song.
- Members of the WSPU were excellent saleswomen and from their shops sold tea caddies and soap, badges, buttons and bags, jewellery and dolls that they had designed and produced.

Civil disobedience by way of tax evasion and refusal to complete census returns was a form of protest used by some. In the 1760s, the American colonists used the slogan 'No taxation without representation' to good effect, and supporters of women's suffrage did not disagree. The Women's Freedom League adopted non-payment of taxes as part of their policy, and several wealthy suffragists had their property seized by bailiffs in lieu of taxes. Censuses were taken every ten years from 1801 in order to enable governments to plan ahead. Both the NUWSS and the WSPU endorsed a boycott of the 1911 census, and hundreds of women made arrangements to be where the enumerator could not count them on census night.

Attacks on property were orchestrated by Christabel Pankhurst for the WSPU and began a new, militant stage in their campaign.

- After 1909, these attacks included pouring acid on golf greens, setting light to the content of pillar boxes and making arson attacks on the homes of prominent politicians.
- After 1912, the attacks intensified: suffragettes smashed the windows of London shops, the Home Office, the Foreign Office and a whole range of government and civil service buildings. An important painting in the National Gallery, the *Rokeby Venus* by Velasquez, was slashed by a suffragette. In 1913, David Lloyd George's house in Surrey was partly destroyed by suffragette arson.

What was the general impact of the suffragette campaign?

- Militancy attracted publicity, and the cause of female emancipation was never far from the newspapers and news bulletins. This publicity attracted funds and recruits.
- Militancy drove those who supported female enfranchisement, but abhorred violence, into the arms of the NUWSS. At the same time, the NUWSS reorganised itself and began a recruiting drive. Membership of the NUWSS grew from 12,000 in 1909 to 50,000 in 1914.
- Militancy drove the anti-suffragists to organise themselves. For example, the National League for Opposing Women's Suffrage was founded in 1911.

HEINEMANN ADVANCED HISTORY

- Militancy convinced those opposed to women's suffrage that women were not to be trusted with the responsibility of the vote.

HOW DID THE LIBERAL GOVERNMENTS (1906–14) RESPOND TO THE SUFFRAGE CAMPAIGNS?

The Liberal government, with its landslide victory in 1906, clearly had the power to enfranchise women. Indeed, with the fresh thinking and new approaches of 'New Liberalism' it might have been expected that female suffrage would be high on the government's agenda. So why wasn't it?

- Prime Minister Herbert Asquith was opposed to votes for women.
- A series of elections and by-elections had eaten away at the government's majority and, from 1910, it relied on support from Irish Nationalist and Labour MPs. The Irish Nationalists were opposed to votes for women and the Labour Party maintained that the enfranchisement of all men had to come first.
- The government had more pressing issues with which to deal: industrial unrest, clashes with the House of Lords and political turmoil in Ireland.

But were these reasons or excuses?

Failed legislation
The parliamentary Liberal Party and the Liberal government did seem ambivalent about granting women the right to vote.

- 1906 the government refused to support an amendment to a plural voting bill that would have enfranchised some women property owners
- 1907 the Commons rejected a women's suffrage bill
- 1908 the Commons passed a women's suffrage bill which was carried on the second reading but rejected ultimately because of Asquith's opposition
- 1910 the first conciliation bill, giving property-owning women the vote, carried, but ultimately failed

because the government refused to give it parliamentary time

- 1911 the second conciliation bill carried, but Asquith announced that he preferred to support universal male suffrage, which could include an amendment for the enfranchisement of women
- 1913 government franchise bill introduced universal male suffrage but an amendment to enfranchise women was declared unconstitutional.

The NUWSS and the WSPU joined forces and worked with the conciliation committees on the 1910 and 1911 bills. The WSPU even suspended all militant activity – but resumed it with increased ferocity when it became clear the bills had failed because of lack of government support. Most of those supporting the campaign for women's suffrage came to believe that the Liberal government wasn't just ambivalent, it was downright hostile to giving votes to women.

Attitudes and actions

The perceived hostility of the government to the enfranchisement of women was borne out by its reaction to the campaigns for women's suffrage.

- When the WSPU began its militant campaign, the government forbade its members to attend Liberal Party meetings unless they had signed tickets. It refused to meet WSPU delegations, banned its meetings in public places, prosecuted the printer who produced *The Suffragette* and forced Christabel Pankhurst to flee to France. It could well be argued that the government denied the proper forms of democratic protest to the suffragettes.
- Initially, imprisoned suffragettes were regarded as political prisoners; they were allowed to wear their own clothes and receive food parcels. From 1908, law-breaking suffragettes were treated as ordinary criminals. In protest, many imprisoned suffragettes resorted to hunger strikes. At first, hunger strikers were released from prison. Later, in order to keep them alive and to refuse them a martyr's death, the government ordered them to be force-fed through their nostrils, mouth and,

sometimes, rectum and vagina. Over 1000 women were treated in this way. The 1913 Prisoners' Discharge Act allowed hunger-striking prisoners to be released, but rearrested once they had regained their strength. Hunger striking was, in many ways, a form of propaganda. It kept the issue of votes for women in the media, gained a lot of sympathy and turned many against the government and its 'Cat and Mouse Act'.

• Winston Churchill was Home Secretary during the reported police brutality of 'Black Friday' on 18 November 1910. Home Secretaries have the ultimate authority over the police and many believed that, though not condoning the violence, Churchill could have stopped it or at least made his disapproval clear, by taking disciplinary action against offending officers.

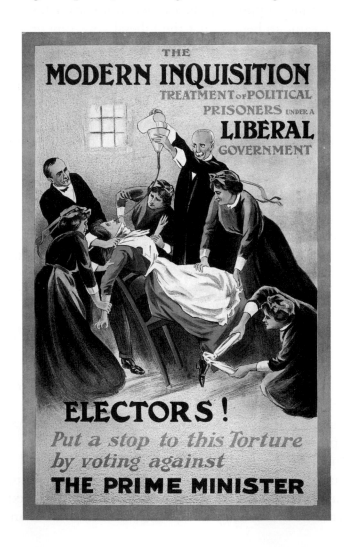

A poster produced by the WSPU in 1910, urging people to vote against the Liberal government

**Sylvia Pankhurst
(1882–1960)** The younger
daughter of Richard and
Emmeline Pankhurst, Sylvia
studied at the Manchester
Municipal School of Art and
Royal College of Art in
London. Involved with the
WSPU, she designed banners,
publications and campaign-
specific items. She organised
the East London Federation
of Suffragettes, an off-shoot of
the WSPU, dedicated to
working-class women. By
campaigning on class lines
and forming a 'People's Army'
to combat class oppression,
Sylvia drew support from
large sections of the male
working class – dockers,
firemen and postal workers.
She also fell foul of the
WSPU leadership and was
expelled by her sister in
January 1914. On the
outbreak of war she founded
the pacifist socialist journal
Worker's Dreadnought and
became a member of the
Women's International
League for Peace. She
campaigned throughout the
war for women's suffrage,
setting up clinics and
nurseries, finding work for
unemployed women and
organising servicemen's wives
to fight for better pensions.
After the war she travelled to
Russia to meet Lenin and
throughout the rest of her life
campaigned for the oppressed.
She died in Ethiopia, where
she had been campaigning for
Ethiopian independence.

This attitude to law-breaking suffragettes was in stark
contrast to the government's attitude to law-breaking over
the problem of Home Rule for Ireland. In this case, the
government turned a blind eye to the law-breaking Ulster
Unionists (see page 98) who remained immune from arrest
and who were consulted over the future of the island of
Ireland.

The turn of the tide?

While the militancy of the WSPU was keeping the issue of
votes for women in the forefront of the public's mind, the
NUWSS was working hard behind the scenes.

- Both the NUWSS and the WSPU feared that they
  would get nothing by way of concessions from the
  Liberal government. The NUWSS therefore made a pact
  with the Labour Party whereby the NUWSS set up an
  electoral fighting fund to support Labour candidates in
  constituencies where they were fighting candidates who
  were opposed to women's suffrage. Between 1912 and
  1914, several Liberals failed to get elected because of
  NUWSS support for their Labour opponents.
- This put pressure on the Liberal government at a time
  when it had lost its overall majority.
- In 1913, Asquith met deputations from the NUWSS.
- In 1914, Asquith met a deputation from **Sylvia
  Pankhurst**'s East London Federation of Suffragettes, and
  hinted that he had it in mind to agree to votes for
  women on the same basis as an extension of the male
  franchise.
- There is evidence to suggest that the Liberal Party was
  pressurising prospective MPs to support women's
  suffrage and seemed to be about to make it part of its
  election manifesto.

BUT all question of enfranchising women ended with the
outbreak of war in August 1914.

WHY WERE WOMEN ENFRANCHISED IN 1918?

The first, most important step towards women's suffrage
was taken after the First World War – a war in which

women played an important part – and so it is tempting to see the war as the turning point in changing the hearts and minds of those previously opposed to votes for women. Is this necessarily so?

- It was generally accepted among politicians that there was a need to reform the franchise. To this end an all-party conference, known as the Speaker's Conference, met behind closed doors in 1916 to discuss franchise reform. Many conference members were known to be sympathetic to the cause of women's suffrage and when the Speaker's Conference submitted its report to Parliament, it recommended that 'some measure of woman suffrage should be conferred' on 'women who have attained a certain age', suggesting 30 or 35 as being appropriate.
- The fear that the enfranchisement of women would benefit one political party over another had largely vanished. Liberal and Labour politicians felt that the social mix in such a large group of women would not lead them necessarily to vote Conservative; Conservatives believed that most women over the age of 30 were likely to be moderate in their voting habits and so they had nothing to lose by agreeing to their enfranchisement.
- In 1915, the Liberal government became a coalition government, and so there was a greater likelihood of cross-party agreement to any decision to enfranchise women.
- The government itself, by 1916/17, contained many more MPs who were sympathetic to the cause. Andrew Bonar Law and Arthur Henderson were promoted to the cabinet, replacing men who were antagonistic. David Lloyd George, a sympathiser, replaced the antagonistic Asquith in 1916 as Prime Minister.
- The cessation of WSPU militancy, for the duration of the war, and the universally acknowledged important contribution of women to the war effort, allowed many MPs (including Asquith) to change their minds without loss of face. Indeed, in 1917, Asquith explained to the House of Commons:

Why, and in what sense, the House may ask, have I changed my views? My opposition to women suffrage has always been based on considerations of public expediency. I think that some years ago I ventured to use the expression 'Let the women work out their own salvation.' Well, Sir, they have. How could we have carried on the War without women? There is hardly a service in which women have not been at least as active as men, and wherever we turn we see them doing work which three years ago would have been regarded as falling exclusively within the province of men. But what moves me more in this matter is the problem of reconstruction when the War is over. The questions which will arise with regard to women's labour and women's functions are questions in which I find it impossible to withhold from women the right of making their voices heard. And let me add that, since the War began, we have had no recurrence of that detestable campaign which disfigured the annals of political agitation in this country, and no one can now contend that we are yielding to violence what we refused to concede to argument.

The Representation of the People Act, that became law in February 1918, gave the right to vote in parliamentary elections to all men over the age of 21 and to all women over the age of 30 who were on the local government register or who were married to men on the local government register.

Like most reform acts that drew lines in the sand, there was no logical reason why women should not, then, have been given the vote on the same terms as men. Perhaps the biggest illogicality was that those women who had risked most and contributed most to the war effort were not themselves enfranchised. Indeed, it could well be argued that the First World War delayed rather than speeded up women's suffrage. But the fact remains that the Act was a compromise – a compromise that was acceptable to all the main parties to the debate, including the WSPU and NUWSS.

SUMMARY QUESTIONS

1 To what extent would you agree with the view that the Liberal governments, 1906–14, were generally unsympathetic to giving women the vote?

2 Did militancy do more harm than good to the cause of women's suffrage?

3 How important was Herbert Asquith in the fight for women's suffrage?

4 How significant was the First World War in gaining the franchise for women?

CHAPTER 6

Industrial unrest

The repeal of the Combination Acts in 1824 made it possible for working people to combine together to press their employers to improve their working conditions or raise their wages. The early unions, apart from Robert Owen's ill-fated Grand National Consolidated Trades Union, tended to be small and localised. However, the 1860s and subsequent years saw the growth of national unions for skilled artisans. These new unions prided themselves on their respectability and, because their members had specialist skills wanted by their employers, usually tended to gain improved conditions by negotiation.

In the 1880s, a different kind of union emerged. Members of these unions were drawn from the unskilled and semi-skilled workforce. They were large and they were militant. Their leaders were men like Will Thorne, Ben Tillet and Tom Mann. They were influenced by socialist ideas and they were not afraid to use the strike weapon. It was these unions that were more readily influenced by **syndicalist** ideas that crossed the Atlantic from the USA in about 1910. Syndicalists believed that ownership and control of industry should be by the workers themselves. They looked for a progressive weakening of capitalist employers by industrial aggression, and considered factory floor action more effective than parliamentary processes.

It is against this background that the unrest that characterised British industry after 1910 must be considered.

STRIKES AND LOCK-OUTS, 1910–14

The years 1910–14 were characterised by serious and sustained industrial unrest. Strikes and lock-outs were not uncommon in industrial Britain, but the wave of strikes that started in 1910 was accompanied by bitterness and

KEY GROUP

Syndicalists They believed that a revolution would bring about socialism. They believed that this revolution would come about through the trade unions because it was the trade unions that had the power to bring down their employers. The key to the revolution was industrial action, culminating in a general strike that would lead to a collapse and workers' control over the economy and society.

violence on an unprecedented scale. These were the most important:

November 1910–October 1911: the miners' strike in South Wales

The grievances that triggered the strike stemmed from a dispute over wages for working difficult and abnormal seams in the coal pits. In November 1910, some miners refused the pay that was offered by their **conciliation board** and 800 miners were locked out. Riots and violence were common, as striking miners tried to persuade colleagues to join them. The worst riots were in Tonypandy. The chief constable of Glamorgan asked Home Secretary Winston Churchill to send in troops to restore law and order. Churchill refused, fearing that the presence of the army on the streets of Tonypandy would only inflame matters. He garrisoned soldiers in Cardiff and Swindon, and sent 300 extra police from London to the Rhondda valleys. During a 'battle' at Tonypandy, one striker died and over 500 were injured. A myth grew up that Churchill had sent troops to kill innocent Welsh miners, and he never again had any sort of following in South Wales. By the spring of 1911, 30,000 miners were on strike. Destitution forced them back to work in October 1911, on the mine owners' terms.

August 1911: the railway workers' strike

The first ever national railway workers' strike was called in August 1911. As with the miners, this was because they

Striking miners in Tonypandy, 1910/11

refused a pay offer determined by their conciliation board. However, this time the government intervened. The strike was settled in two days, largely because of the intervention and negotiating skills of Lloyd George. And it was settled in the union's favour.

The triple alliance

Encouraged by the success of the railway workers, the Miners' Federation called a national strike for February 1912, demanding a minimum wage. Again the government intervened and accepted the principle of a minimum wage, though the rate was not as high as the miners had hoped. The dockers' strike that followed was less successful. Ports were scattered throughout the country and dockers had little sense of national solidarity. Although the government intervened, it was unable to find a solution and the strike collapsed, largely because it lacked the support of other workers.

But that support was forthcoming two years later. In order to increase their bargaining power, dockers, miners and railwaymen formed a 'triple alliance' in 1914. Trade union membership (see table below) was now topping 4 million and industrial strife was reaching a climax – when the First World War intervened to create a truce in all forms of industrial unrest.

Year	Total union membership in millions	Number of stoppages	Total working days lost in millions
1906	2.2	479	3.0
1907	2.5	585	2.1
1908	2.5	389	10.8
1909	2.5	422	2.7
1910	2.5	521	9.9
1911	3.1	872	10.1
1912	3.4	834	40.9
1913	4.1	1459	9.8
1914	4.1	972	9.9

Trade unionism and industrial unrest, 1906–14

Why was there so much industrial unrest at this time?

Towards the end of the 1890s, a period of falling prices had given way to inflation, and, under the Liberals, the economy began to expand again. By 1911, unemployment had fallen to 3 per cent. So why was there so much discontent on the industrial front?

- The 1906 Trades Disputes Act (see page 21) removed the restraint that unions were legally liable for costs incurred to their employers as a result of a strike, and the accumulated grievances of working people combined to prompt widespread industrial action.
- Many unions amalgamated into federations such as the Miners Federation. This gave them more power and gave any stoppages a much greater impact.
- Industrial workers had looked to the Labour Party to right their wrongs. In this they were disappointed and there were several reasons for this:
  - Labour MPs in Parliament were a small group. Only 42 Labour MPs remained after the two elections of 1910 and, lacking parliamentary experience, their influence on the Liberal government was slight.
  - After 1910, the Labour Party (led by Ramsay MacDonald) found itself supporting Liberal legislation rather than initiating reforms that would help the working class.
  - The **Osborne judgement** of 1909 meant that the Labour Party was chronically underfunded, even though payment of salaries (£400 per annum) to MPs was introduced in 1911.
  - The Labour Party was unhappy with the Old Age Pensions Act and the National Insurance Act. Its unhappiness is best expressed by the social historian and Labour Party supporter R. H. Tawney, writing in 1912:

    The middle and upper class view of social reform is that it should regulate the worker's life in order that he may work better. The working class view of economic reform is that it should regulate his work in order that he may live better. Hence to working people, insurance acts and pensions etc. seem to be beginning at the wrong end.

KEY JUDGEMENT

The Osborne judgement
In 1908, a railway employee called Walter Osborne took legal action to prevent his union giving financial support to a political party of which he did not approve. The case went as far as the House of Lords, who found in his favour in 1909. The main effect of this judgement was to limit Labour Party funds. The situation for the Labour Party didn't improve until 1913, when legislation made it possible for it again to take money from the unions by giving individuals the right to opt out of the 'political levy'.

However, the Parliamentary Labour Party was not strong enough to propose alternative legislation.
- The Labour Party was itself divided about how far it should adopt socialism and what its relationship should be with the trade union movement.

As a result of their disappointment with the Labour Party, working-class people began to take direct action by way of strikes.

• Collective bargaining did not always work: decisions of the national conciliation boards were frequently found to be unacceptable by workers in the regions. This was because often they did not address local grievances. Because of this, local trade union officials were frequently at odds with the leaders of their unions at national level. Furthermore, not all the workforce was unionised. In 1910, for example, only about 17 per cent of industrial workers belonged to a union. Thus, the non-unionised workforce did not feel itself in any way bound by decisions made by a conciliation board comprising employers and union officials.

• The workforce, by 1912, was far better educated than in the previous century. There was an increasing awareness of inequalities of income, heightened by the publication of the reports of Booth and Rowntree (see pages 36–37) which were summarised in the popular press. The author H. G. Wells wrote in 1912:

> *The old workman might, and did, quarrel very vigorously with his own employer, but he never set out to find fault with all employers. He wanted an extra shilling or he wanted an hour of leisure and that was as much as he wanted. The young workman, on the other hand, has put the whole social system on trial and seems quite disposed to give an adverse verdict. He looks far beyond the older conflict of interests between employer and employed.*

• In some areas and in some industries, people with syndicalist views were agitating the workers. The union leader Tom Mann, who had been one of the instigators of the London dock strike of 1889, launched a newspaper *The Industrial Syndicalist* in 1910. In it he propounded his view about how the workers could win control of the state. After one of his speeches in 1911, a Liverpool crowd attacked soldiers and police and, in the general riot, two demonstrators were killed.

Some miners in South Wales set out their syndicalist views in a pamphlet called *The Miners' Next Step*, published in 1912. The pamphlet called for a minimum wage and a seven-hour working day.

> We cannot get rid of our employers and slave-driving in the mining industry, until all other industries have been organised for, and progressed toward, the same objective. All we can do is set an example and the pace.

> Our objective begins to take shape before your eyes. Every industry thoroughly organised, in the first place, to fight, to gain control of, and then to administer, that industry. The co-ordination of all industries on a Central Production Board, who, with a statistical department to ascertain the needs of the people, will issue its demands on the different departments of industry, leaving the men themselves to determine under what conditions and how, the work should be done. This would mean real democracy in real life, making for real manhood and womanhood. Any other form of democracy is a delusion and a snare.

While syndicalism clearly played a part in the industrial unrest in the years immediately before the First World War, it tended to agitate grievances that were already there.

Was Britain on the verge of civil war, 1910–14?

Many contemporaries did fear that industrial anarchy was just around the corner. In reality, horrific and frightening though the industrial violence must have been, civil war was unlikely.

- Although the Liberal government's welfare reforms were not universally popular, no one wanted them torn up. Indeed, there was pressure for them to be extended.
- Middle-class jobs, in the civil service and other professional and administrative occupations, were growing. Since 1891, they had increased by just over 40 per cent for men and for women. In 1911, just under 25

per cent of employed people in Britain were in middle-class occupations and the rate was rising. It was the middle classes that gave stability to British society, and it was these middle classes that did not want to destabilise the security of the state. Equally, many working-class workers and voters did not want industrial strife, and almost a third of those who could vote, voted for the Conservative Party.

- The electorate seemed to disapprove of militancy: the Labour Party did badly in by-elections after 1910. Indeed, Labour politicians were busy trying to forge an alliance with the Liberals and it was, at the time, difficult to see them as a viable alternative government.

The bitter industrial strife, coupled with the constitutional conflict with the House of Lords and the increasing militancy of the suffragettes after the failure of the conciliation bills, made the four years prior to the outbreak of war in 1914 ones of particular stress for the Liberal government. The outbreak of war in August 1914 did not solve any of the problems that were facing the government; it simply put them on hold until the war was over.

SUMMARY QUESTIONS

1 How far do you agree with the view that the weakness of the Labour Party was the main cause of industrial unrest between 1910 and 1914?

2 To what extent was Britain facing civil war in the years 1910–14?

3 The Liberal government faced constitutional, economic and social crises in the years from 1909. Explain whether or not this means it was a weak government.

THE FIRST WORLD WAR AT A GLANCE

Year	Western Front	Eastern Front	Other Fronts
1914	German armies advance through Belgium. **August:** Battle of Mons. **September:** Battle of the Marne. Schlieffen plan halted. **October-November:** Armies race for the sea. Trench warfare follows.	**August:** German armies victorious over Russians at Battle of Tanneberg and in **September:** Masurian Lakes.	**November:** British forces occupy Basra on the Persian Gulf as part of the war against Turkey.
1915	**April-May:** Germans use chlorine gas at the Battle of Ypres. **Autumn:** British and French offensives comes to little.	**May-September:** Huge offensive by German army in Galicia results in the Russian army retreating 300 miles and losing 1,000,000 soldiers. **September:** Russian commander Grand Duke Nicholas Nicholaievich replaced by Tsar Nicholas II.	War against Turkey – British forces advance on Baghdad but are forced back to Kut. **March:** Dardanelles campaign begins. **April:** Treaty of London promises parts of the Austrian Empire to Italy in exchange for joining the war. British troops conquer the Cameroons. South Africans invade German South West Africa. Fighting in East Africa.
1916	**February:** Battle of Verdun begins. **July:** Anglo-French forces attempt to relieve pressure on Verdun at the Battle of the Somme.	**September:** Advances by Russian General halted by 15 German divisions from the Western Front. Russian army loses another 1,000,000 men.	**January:** Dardanelles campaign halted. **April:** British troops in Kut forced to surrender. Russians launch a campaign against the Turks in Armenia. General Smuts pushes Germans back in East Africa.
1917	**April:** Failed French offensive at Chemin des Dames. **May:** Mutiny breaks out in the French ranks involving half of the army. British offensive at third Battle of Ypres (Passchendaele). No breakthrough in horrific conditions.	**February:** Tsar abdicates, replaced by a Provisional Government. **Summer:** Disastrous Galician campaign. **October:** Bolshevik revolution. **December:** Peace negotiations with Germans at the Polish town of Brest-Litovsk.	**April:** USA declares war on Germany. **October:** Italian line breaks at the Battle of Caporetto. Situation stabilised with help from British and French reinforcements. Over 300,000 troops lost. **December:** British take Jerusalem from the Turks.
1918	**March-April:** Germans launch huge offensive. Initially successful, then halted due to lack of reserves and supplies. **May-June:** German offensive in the Champagne region halted by French/American troops. **August:** Battles of the Marne and Amiens; Allies on the offensive. Germans are pushed back towards the border. **11 November:** Hostilities cease at 11 o'clock.	**March:** Treaty of Brest-Litovsk. Russians forced to sign away huge areas of land including the Baltic States, the Ukraine and Finland. Russian collapse in the East.	**Summer:** The Austro-Hungarian Empire disintegrates. **September:** British break Turkish lines in Palestine, helped by Arab forces led by T.E. Lawrence (Lawrence of Arabia). **October-November:** Italians break through at the Battle of Vitorio Veneto. **November:** Allied fleet arrives at Constantinople.

The war in the air and at sea	The British Home Front
War at sea: **August:** British and French navies blockade Central Powers. **December:** German Pacific Fleet defeated by British Fleet at the Battle of the Falkland Islands. German battleships bombard Scarborough and Hartlepool.	**August:** The Defence of the Realm Act (DORA). The government takes over the railways. **September:** Recruiting campaign begins. **December:** Union of Democratic Control set up by those opposing the war.
War at sea: **January:** Naval skirmish at Dogger Bank. Result inconclusive. German submarine campaign in the Atlantic. **May:** The liner *Lusitania* is sunk. **War in the air:** Germans try to draw the Royal Flying Corps back to Britain by bombing targets on the British mainland. Fifteen Zeppelin raids on British towns.	**May:** Coalition government replaces the Liberal government. Munitions Act gives the government power to take direct control of munitions factories. **June:** War Committee is set up. **July:** Ministry of Munitions is set up. National Registration Act Act registers men eligible for military service. **October:** British nurse Edith Cavell is executed by the Germans.
War at sea: **31 May/1 June:** Battle of Jutland. Result inconclusive **War in the air:** **April:** French introduce the Nieuport 3 and Spad 3 planes. The British unveil the Sopwith Camel. 41 Zeppelin raids against England.	**January:** Conscription is introduced. **April:** Easter Uprising in Dublin by those who want Irish Independence. **December:** Lloyd George becomes prime minister.
War at sea: Submarine war against Allied shipping intensifies. Introduction of convoy system in the second half of the year reduces losses considerably.	**February:** Bread rationed, voluntary rationing of other foods food shortages increase. Government guarantees prices of basic food. Women's Land Army created. Air raids continue against towns on the east coast.
War at sea: Repeated naval raids on the British coast. **June:** German fleet scuttled at Scapa Flow. In June 1919, the German sailors sink their own fleet when it is under guard at Scapa Flow. **November:** Following the armistice the German fleet surrenders to the British at Rosyth.	**February:** Women over 30 are given the vote for the first time. **March:** Ministry of Information created to improve morale. **April:** Meat rationing introduced. **July:** Education Act raises the school leaving age.

HEINEMANN ADVANCED HISTORY

CHAPTER 7

The challenge of the Home Front 1914–18: the state and the politicians

At the outbreak of war, all political parties pledged their support to the government. On 2 August, the Conservatives committed themselves to the government; John Redmond and the Irish Nationalists followed two days later; on 5 August, the Labour Party followed suit. There were some exceptions, but these tended to be isolated individuals opposed to the war on principle. So, within the first few days of the declaration of war, a united Commons supported the Liberal government in whatever it was going to do as it took the country over the brink and into the abyss.

EARLY DAYS AND FALSE STARTS

Initially, Asquith, as Prime Minister, conducted the war through the normal processes and procedures of party government. This simply didn't work. A cabinet of some 20 members was far too big to take instant decisions and respond rapidly to changing circumstances. Decisions were taken by the few ministers who could be called together at short notice. There was little overall strategy and planning – just reaction to events. The only new member of the cabinet was Lord Kitchener, Secretary of State for War (see page 80): he struggled to come to terms with the demands of his new post and the problems posed by trench warfare. His lack of decisiveness and inability to grasp the wider scene fatally undermined Asquith's position, already weakened by the apparent inability of the major cabinet players to pull together.

- Herbert Asquith himself, although intellectually powerful, lacked the ability to make quick decisions and carry them through.
- Winston Churchill, full of daring, developed impractical schemes that cost hundreds of lives such as the Dardanelles campaign of 1915.

Munitions Military weapons, ammunition, equipment and stores.

John French (1852–1925)
A charismatic cavalry officer during the second Boer War (1899–1902), he was promoted steadily and in 1912 became Chief of the Imperial General Staff. In 1914, he commanded the British forces in France. Weak at both staff work and diplomacy, his relations with the French were poor. His reaction to the failures of trench warfare was to keep on sending men 'over the top' to their deaths. He then secretly encouraged *The Times* and the *Daily Mail* to blame Kitchener for not supplying him with enough shells and the subsequent scandal nearly brought him down. After another disaster at Loos, he was replaced in December 1915 by Douglas Haig. Sir John French spent the rest of the war as commander-in-chief of the Home Forces. After the war, he was (1918–21) Lord Lieutenant of Ireland where he totally failed to understand the complexities of Irish nationalism. In 1922, he was given a peerage as the 1st Earl of Ypres, a gesture that was not necessarily intended to be ironic.

- David Lloyd George was impatient with the lack of decisiveness and direction in the cabinet, and certain he could do better than all of them.

Lloyd George and the shell scandal

In the spring of 1915, matters came to a head with the first effective challenge to Asquith's leadership.

- On 22 February, Lloyd George circulated his colleagues with a memorandum arguing that the whole economy had to be geared up for total war and that this meant reorganising factories and engineering works to focus on the production of **munitions**. In this way, he argued, Britain would be able to equip its own armed forces and those of its allies. This was in direct opposition to Kitchener, who wanted to continue with the existing War Office contracts. The battle between the two men carried on throughout April and May.
- The shortage of shells on the Western Front was brought to the attention of the public by the publication on 14 May in *The Times* of a telegram from its war correspondent, Major Charles Repington. Part of the telegram read:

  We had not sufficient high explosives to lower the enemy's parapets to the ground, after the French practice. The infantry did splendidly, but the conditions were too bad. The want of an unlimited supply of high explosives was a fatal bar to our success.

  Sir John French, commander-in-chief of the British forces, had previously assured Kitchener that he had all the ammunition he needed, although this wasn't known until long afterwards. Here was crisis indeed.
- Sir John Fisher, the First Sea Lord, resigned on 15 May. His reason was that he could no longer work with Winston Churchill, the First Lord of the Admiralty, who was determined to increase the naval forces at Gallipoli at the expense of the Home Fleet.

Asquith's government was now fatally compromised. He could no longer depend upon Conservative support and was forced to look for a formal coalition government rather than rely upon informal agreements between the major parties.

DELIVERING THE GOODS.

'Delivering the Goods': this cartoon was published in *Punch* in April 1915

KEY PERSON

Douglas Haig (1861-1928)
Believed to be the best soldier of his generation, his reputation was ruined during the First World War. He took over from Sir John French in December 1915 as Commander-in-Chief of the British forces on the Western Front. The British army suffered tremendous losses at the Somme and at the third battle of Ypres because of Haig's theory that Germany would run out of men before the allies did. The horrors of this part of the war overshadowed his undoubted successes between August and September 1918 when the German army's resistance was broken at Amiens and in the 'Hundred Days' battles. Strongly supported by some political leaders and by King George V, he and Lloyd George loathed each other. After the war, he devoted himself to the welfare of ex-servicemen, setting up the Haig Fund with its Poppy Day appeal. He remains a controversial figure: some historians regard him as a 'butcher', others as an educated man of limited ability.

THE ASQUITH COALITION GOVERNMENT

Andrew Bonar law, the leader of the Conservative Party, was in a strong position. Asquith needed him and his party's support more than he needed Asquith. Bonar Law was able to dictate his own terms and these included the removal of Churchill from the Admiralty. Bonar Law became Colonial Secretary; Balfour replaced Churchill at the Admiralty; and Lloyd George took over the newly created Ministry of Munitions. The last Liberal government of the twentieth century had come to an end.

The coalition government, however, was no stronger than the previous Liberal government under Asquith. Direction of the war remained hesitant, piecemeal and fraught by disagreements among members of the government. The issues that divided them were those of **conscription** and whether or not to create a smaller war cabinet which would be responsible to the larger cabinet for the conduct of the war.

KEY TERM

Conscription The enforcing of men to join the armed services and fight for their country.

Why was conscription a problem?

Although Kitchener's campaign to recruit men into the armed forces on a voluntary basis was a success, as losses grew it became clear that, if the British army was to be maintained at full fighting strength, some form of conscription would have to be introduced.

- Lloyd George argued that without conscription the war could not be won. However, most Liberals were uneasy at this element of compulsion which went against their traditional principles of independence and individual freedom.
- Asquith suggested a compromise whereby the whole adult male population registered for service, but would not actually be conscripted into the armed forces.
- Asquith's compromise ended in failure: by December 1915, recruitment had fallen to 55,000 per month and conscription was introduced in January 1916. Sir John Simon, the Home Secretary, appalled at this retreat from everything the Liberals stood for, resigned.

Why was the creation of a war cabinet a problem?

Initially, the war was conducted disastrously by the whole cabinet which was far too big for quick and effective decision-making. A committee, put together originally to consider the Dardanelles campaign, became an official war committee in November 1915. It had nine members and proper records were kept of its meetings. But it was a committee without power and therefore without effectiveness. It became little more than a talking shop. Then two events brought matters to a head:

- In July 1916, Lord Kitchener was sent on a mission to Russia. His ship, *HMS Hampshire*, struck a mine as it rounded Scapa Flow in the Orkneys, and Kitchener was drowned.
- David Lloyd George was appointed Minister for War in Kitchener's place.

The end of the Asquith coalition

Lloyd George finally took decisive action:

- On 1 December 1916, he proposed the formation of a small war cabinet consisting of himself, Andrew Bonar Law (Conservative) and Edward Carson (Ulster Unionist). Herbert Asquith would remain as Prime Minister but would not take part in the war cabinet.
- This wasn't just a suggestion from out of the blue. Lloyd George had discussed the matter previously with Bonar Law and Carson.

Asquith was at first inclined to dismiss the whole suggestion out of hand. Then, with the threat of Conservative resignations, he began to change his mind and on 3 December accepted Lloyd George's proposal. But that wasn't the end of the matter.

- On 4 December, an article in *The Times* commented on the proposal in a way that put Asquith in a bad light.
- Asquith changed his mind, saying that he 'would not be relegated to the position of an irresponsible spectator of the War'.
- Lloyd George resigned from the Asquith coalition.
- All the Conservative ministers resigned from the Asquith coalition.
- And finally, on 5 December, Asquith resigned.

On 6 December, a conference of the party leaders was held at Buckingham Palace. It was attended by Asquith and Lloyd George (Liberal), Bonar Law and Balfour (Conservative) and Arthur Henderson (Labour).

- Andrew Bonar Law was offered the post of Prime Minister. He said he would accept only if Asquith agreed to serve under him.
- Asquith refused.

It gradually emerged that Conservative ministers would agree to serve in a government that was led by David Lloyd George.

A NON-PARTY MANDATE.

JOHN BULL. "I DON'T CARE WHO LEADS THE COUNTRY SO LONG AS HE LEADS IT TO VICTORY."

- On 7 December 1916, a very reluctant King George V offered the post of Prime Minister to Lloyd George.
- Lloyd George accepted.
- Herbert Asquith and other Liberal ministers resigned from the government.
- Liberal MPs continued to recognise Asquith as their party leader, but pledged themselves to support the king's government in the conduct of the war.
- Lloyd George secured the support of Conservative and Labour MPs as well as about 100 Liberal MPs.

While Lloyd George remained Prime Minister for the rest of the war, Herbert Asquith remained leader of the Liberal Party. Many Liberals viewed Lloyd George's actions as little short of treachery. Certainly, the Liberal Party remained divided for many years and never again formed a government. This is dealt with in greater detail and depth in Chapter 10.

WHAT WAS THE EFFECT OF DAVID LLOYD GEORGE'S PREMIERSHIP?

The most immediate effect of Lloyd George taking on the role of prime minister was that the conduct of the war became invigorated. Indeed, this change of attitude was sorely needed. By the end of 1916, losses on the Western Front had risen horrifically; by the following spring, U-boat warfare threatened to bring Britain to its knees. Morale among civilians and troops was at an all-time low. Never afraid of new ideas and approaches, Lloyd George injected into the situation a dynamism and a will to win that had been lacking under the vacillating direction of Asquith.

Lloyd George immediately appointed a war cabinet. This consisted of himself, Bonar Law, Lord Curzon, Lord Milner and Arthur Henderson. Arthur Balfour became Foreign Secretary and Edward Carson, First Lord of the Admiralty. This war cabinet met on a more or less daily basis and remained firmly in command of the direction of the war.

However, Lloyd George was not without his critics:

- The military high command objected to a politician directing aspects of strategy and tactics. Lloyd George countered this by maintaining that the vast numbers of men and quantity of materials demanded by the military meant that the military had to be accountable to government and that the government had to be involved in their deployment. This belief led to Lloyd George, for example, refusing to send 18-year-olds into the trenches on the Western Front and insisting that the Admiralty order a convoy system to protect merchant ships bringing vital supplies to Britain. The friction between the military chiefs and Lloyd George continued throughout the war.
- Between December 1916 and the end of the war in November 1918, Lloyd George rarely attended Parliament. He was simply too busy with the direction of the war through the war cabinet. As a consequence of this, he relied more and more on outside experts to advise him on specific aspects of running both the

country and the war. These experts were not accountable to Parliament because they were not elected. Lloyd George's critics claimed he was abandoning the traditional methods of parliamentary government. Some went so far as to suggest he was becoming an American-style president or even a dictator.

To these critics, Lloyd George replied simply that, in wartime

> *a perfectly democratic state has the right to commandeer every resource, every power, life, limb, wealth, and everything else for the interest of the State.*

THE COUPON ELECTION, DECEMBER 1918

As the war drew to a close, it became clear that, after eight years without a general election, the people expected to go to the polls as soon as possible. But the general election, which was eventually held in December 1918, was going to be different for a variety of reasons, the most important of which were the Maurice debate and the Representation of the People Act.

The Maurice debate, May 1918

The final offensive against Germany began in March 1918. Lloyd George, aware that there had been mutterings that he was deliberately keeping troops in Britain to save unnecessary slaughter on the Western Front, announced on 9 April that there were more British troops in France in January 1918 than there had been in January 1917. Less than a month later, this was challenged by General F. D. Maurice, who had only recently retired as director of military operations. He wrote to the press, accusing the government of 'mis-statements' – a polite term for lies.

At this point, Asquith mounted his only public challenge to Lloyd George. Taking the side of the generals, he called for a select committee of enquiry into the matter and proposed a vote of 'no confidence' in the coalition government. In the Commons debate that followed on 9 May, Lloyd George pointed out that the figures he had quoted came from General Maurice's own department, and won the argument by 293 votes to 106. He omitted to say that Maurice's department had sent him corrected figures a couple of days later that virtually destroyed his argument.

On the face of it, this was just a little quarrel between two politicians. But the Maurice debate had far-reaching consequences:

- It destroyed any chance of an immediate Liberal reunification. Ninety-six Liberals had voted with Asquith and against Lloyd George. Asquith had revealed just how deep the differences were between him and Lloyd George and the extent to which they divided the Liberal Party.
- It revealed just how dependent Lloyd George was on his Conservative supporters.

The Representation of the People Act 1918

This became law in February 1918 (see page 57) and so the first postwar general election would be fought with women voting for the first time (along with all men over 21). Even though female suffrage was limited, and would remain so until 1928, no one knew quite what effect the women's vote would have on the election result.

Political problems

As 1918 progressed and the war was clearly coming to an end, the political situation was very fluid. Lloyd George headed the coalition government and could claim with justification to have been a successful wartime leader. But what of the peace?

- Lloyd George's split with Asquith meant that he was unlikely, ever, to lead the Liberal Party: Asquith would not give way to him and too many Liberals would not tolerate him as leader of their party. How was Lloyd George to continue in politics?
- The Labour Party had held office in Lloyd George's coalition government and had to decide whether to continue under Lloyd George or to stand for election on their own.

- The Conservatives, too, had to decide whether to support Lloyd George, a Liberal, or end the coalition and fight the election on their own manifesto.

The 'coupons'

Before the actual election, there were various political manoeuvrings:

- The Labour Party decided to leave the coalition and fight the election as a separate party.
- In July, a group of Lloyd George's Liberal MPs met to discuss their future. They wrote to Lloyd George urging him to sign an electoral agreement with the Conservatives.
- By October, an agreement had been reached with Andrew Bonar Law, the Conservative leader, whereby 150 Lloyd George Liberal candidates would not be opposed by Conservatives in the constituencies concerned.
- A letter explaining this, and signed by Lloyd George and Bonar Law, was sent to all candidates who were willing to support the coalition.

Angrily, Asquith nicknamed these 'coupons', referring to the ration card coupons that were used during the war, and the election became known as the 'coupon election'.

Why were these decisions made?

- The Labour Party had had experience of office within the Lloyd George coalition, was in a healthy financial state because of the growth in trade unionism and wanted to test the increased electorate by standing in its own right.
- The Conservatives genuinely admired Lloyd George's leadership skills and believed he was the only person who could unite right-wing politicians against what they saw as the threat from **Bolshevism**.
- To agree to the continuation of the coalition was Lloyd George's only hope of retaining a high profile in British politics.

	Seats won	Total votes	% vote
Coalition Conservative	335	3,504,198	32.6
Coalition Liberal	133	1,445,640	13.5
Coalition Labour	10	161,521	1.5
(Coalition totals)	(478)	(5,111,359)	(47.6)
Labour	63	2,385,472	22.2
Asquithian Liberals	28	1,298,808	12.1
Conservatives	23	370,375	3.4
Irish Unionists	25	292,722	2.7
Irish Nationalists	7	238,477	2.2
Sinn Fein	73	486,867	4.5
Others	17	810,980	8.0

General election results, December 1918

The election

Voting took place on Saturday 14 December. It was the first time the whole country voted on the same day. However, the soldiers overseas voted too, and so it was a fortnight before the results were announced.

The result was, clearly, a triumph for the coalition and for Lloyd George. But what was the long-term impact of the coupon election?

- Lloyd George's decision to carry the coalition into peacetime government split the Liberal Party, making it unelectable.
- The coalition victory in 1918 was significant because it began a four-year period of non-party government. However, it could be seen as
  - a victory for the Conservatives, because the Liberals were hopelessly split and the Labour Party too weak to form a government, but the victory was disguised as Lloyd George remained Prime Minister.
  - The growing 'threat' from Labour was neutralised.

Herbert Gladstone, a former Liberal chief whip, wrote in a private letter in 1919:

The result of 1918 broke the party not only in the House of Commons but also in the country. Local [Liberal] Associations perished or kept up a nominal existence. Masses of our best men passed away to Labour. Others gravitated to

Conservatism or independence. Funds were depleted and we were short of workers all over the country. There was an utter lack of enthusiasm or even zeal.

SUMMARY QUESTIONS

1 Are you surprised at Asquith's performance as a war-time politician?
   (You will need to look back at pages 52–7 as well as using material in this chapter to help you in your answer.)

2 Using the information in this chapter, explain whether or not you believe generals or politicians should run wars.

3 Was David Lloyd George a good wartime leader?

4 Who gained, and who lost, in the 'coupon election'?

5 Do you think David Lloyd George was a hero or a villain?

CHAPTER 8

The challenge of the Home Front 1914–18: the state and the people

The outbreak of war in August 1914 launched the British people into a period when their lives would be shaped by the demands of total war. For the first time, civilians and armed forces would be called upon to commit hearts, nerves and sinews, money, time and their lives to the conflict. This war, because it was fought between highly industrialised nation states, demanded the total commitment of the political, economic and social resources of the countries involved. The national resources – and this included people – of all the combatants had to be mobilised on an unprecedented scale over a period of four years. The efforts of the armed forces would come to nothing if they could not be backed by a civilian population capable of sustaining a high level of industrial output. In order to wage total war, the whole adult population of Britain had to be mobilised effectively and efficiently. How was this done?

CONTROLLING THE PEOPLE: THE STATE INTERVENES

Britain had no written constitution that guaranteed the rights of individuals against an overbearing state and so the government had few problems in passing legislation concerning, for example, conscription. Parliament itself surrendered some of its authority to the government on 8 August when it agreed to the Defence of the Realm Act (DORA). This Act gave the government wide powers 'for securing the public safety and defence of the realm'. Its provisions were extended at various points throughout the war. DORA meant that the government could react quickly to crises, without the long-drawn out procedures and processes of setting up acts of parliament.

What was DORA used for?

DORA included measures to

- prevent anyone obtaining and passing on information likely to benefit an enemy – in other words, spying
- protect important centres of communication: railways, docks and harbours
- facilitate a stream of regulations governing, for example, food rationing and air-raid precautions
- set up a system of press censorship
- detain suspected persons without trial.

MOBILISING THE PEOPLE: THE ARMED FORCES

The first and most obvious need was for soldiers. On 5 August, the House of Commons authorised an increase in the regular army by half a million men.

One of the best-known recruiting posters of the First World War, showing Kitchener's finger pointing at the 'guilty' young men who had not yet joined up

Volunteers

On 7 August, **Lord Kitchener**, the Minister of War, appealed for the first 100,000 volunteers to form the basis of a new army. Recruiting offices up and down the country were swamped as young men, in a fever of patriotic enthusiasm, volunteered to fight for 'King and Country'.

'Pals battalions', formed on the basis of 'those who joined together should serve together', proved an enormously popular move. All kinds of companies and businesses, towns and cities formed their own battalions. Hull raised four battalions; Glasgow, three. Accrington, a small cotton town in Lancashire, raised one in only ten days of recruiting. In Liverpool, the White Star shipping line formed its own platoon as did the Cunard line and the Cotton Exchange. There were artists' battalions and battalions raised by orchestras and other cultural groups. Over 300 battalions, some 250,000 men altogether, were raised in this way. What no one told them was that joining together and serving together also meant dying together, and whole towns were devastated in this way.

There had been no war between the great powers since 1871. Only the elderly knew what war was like and this war, total war, would be profoundly different. No one knew what to expect, but most thought it would be an affair of set battles quickly decided, and would be over by Christmas. They planned accordingly. Kitchener, however, summoned to the cabinet just after the outbreak of war, warned that the war would last at least three years and would need more than 1 million men. He was received in silence. The Foreign Secretary, Edward Grey, said afterwards that he thought the prediction 'unlikely, if not incredible'.

Conscripts

Over 1 million men had signed up by the end of 1914 and, altogether, some 2.5 million men volunteered to fight. But this was not enough. As the losses on the Western Front mounted, and disillusionment with the war grew, it became clear that some sort of conscription would have to be introduced.

KEY TERMS

Reserved occupations
These were occupations that the government thought were so important to the war effort that the workers could not be released for military service.

Conscientious objector A conscientious objector is a person whose conscience will not allow them to fight. During the First World War, conscientious objection was allowed on religious grounds provided the person concerned contributed to the war in other ways. About 7000 served as non-combatants, driving ambulances, for example; 3000 worked in labour camps and a further 6000 were imprisoned because they refused to have anything at all to do with the war effort. There was little sympathy for conscientious objectors: it was common for girls and young women to give white feathers, a sign of cowardice, to men they suspected of being conscientious objectors. Conscientious objectors who failed to convince their tribunal that they had a genuine religious objection to fighting were simply sent to the Front, ready to be court-martialled the first time they refused an order.

Army recruiting in the First World War

- In October 1915, Lord Derby was made director-general of recruiting. He invited all men between the ages of 18 and 41 to attest their willingness to serve. They were to 'attest' in age groups; and a pledge was given that no married men would be called on until there were no more available single men. The 'Derby scheme' was a last-ditch attempt to find recruits before introducing compulsory military service. It failed. Out of 2,179,231 single men of military age who had not previously volunteered to fight, only half came forward to attest.
- In January 1916, the first Conscription Act made military service compulsory for all unmarried men between the ages of 18 and 41.
- In May 1916, a further Conscription Act extended compulsory military service to all men of military age, married or not. The only exceptions allowed were for those men who worked in **reserved occupations** and for **conscientious objectors**.

Were enough men found to fight?

The short answer to this question is 'only just'.

- The poverty and poor nutrition of industrial workers in prewar Britain resulted in large numbers of men failing to reach the minimum standard for military service. In some industrial areas, 70 per cent of men were rejected as unfit.
- Thousands were excluded from conscription on the basis that they were doing important war work on the Home Front, such as engineering, mining and munitions work.

	Total joining the armed forces	Fighting strength of the British army on 1 October each year
1914	1,186,357	1,327,372
1915	1,280,000	2,475,764
1916	1,190,000	3,343,797
1917	820,000	3,883,017
1918	493,562	3,838,265

The huge losses of 1916–17 meant that the size of the army was barely increasing. The German offensive in the spring of 1918 caused 300,000 British casualties and seriously damaged the British army's ability to conduct the war. Desperate measures had to be adopted, including sending 18-year-olds to the trenches in northern France – something the government had previously promised not to do. Indeed, by the end of the war, half the British infantry in France was under 19 years old.

MOBILISING THE PEOPLE: CIVILIANS

Mobilising men into the armed forces was, however, only one part of what had to be done. The remaining workforce had to be mobilised too, so that servicemen and civilians were properly supplied with everything necessary for maintaining life and winning the war. This meant that British industry had to be geared up to intensive production.

- In May 1915, a Munitions of War Act was passed. This put on a legal footing the Treasury Agreement of March 1915, made between the Trades Union Congress (TUC) and the Chancellor of the Exchequer, David Lloyd George. The Act applied to all industries engaged in war work:
  - Strikes and lock-outs were prohibited.
  - All workplace differences were to be 'solved' by compulsory arbitration.
  - Wage rates would be safeguarded and any wage rate increases had to be approved by the government.
  - Trade unions were to abandon restrictive practices and permit unskilled and semi-skilled men and women to take the place of skilled men who were away in the armed services. This was commonly known as 'dilution'.
  - Profits within these 'controlled' industries were to be limited.
  - The government had the power to direct people to work in specific industries in specific parts of the country.
  - People committing offences under this Act were to be tried in special munitions tribunals.

- A Ministry of Munitions was set up in May 1915, with David Lloyd George as its minister. By 1918, it had a staff of 65,000 employing some 3 million workers in over 20,000 factories.
- In August 1915, a national register of all men and women aged between 15 and 65 was compiled. Sunday 15 August was the day set aside for all 'qualifying' adults to provide details of their age and occupation. Lord Lansdowne (a member of the government and Minister without Portfolio) explained that its purpose was to ensure

> *that every member of the community should bear not only a part in the national task, but the part he is best qualified to take.*

Liberals worried at the loss of civil liberties this national registration implied, but, in the context of total war, few complained. In practice, the enormous powers implied by national registration were never fully exercised.

This is one of the posters issued by the government to encourage women to join the workforce. Its message is similar to that of the recruiting poster on page 79. Why do you think the technique used is so different?

Persuasion and propaganda were enough to fill the munitions factories and keep all Britain's basic industries going.

HOW WERE THE COUNTRY'S RESOURCES MANAGED?

Many Liberals, wedded to the ideas of free trade and individualism, found it difficult to come to terms with the deliberate state intervention that was essential during total war. Ideas about a free market had to be put to one side, and it seemed to many that the ideals for which they had been arguing for most of their political life had suddenly become worthless.

Industry

The government had potentially draconian powers to control the production and distribution of raw materials and manufactured goods. However, it rarely had to use them. In theory, the government was able to requisition whatever it wanted. However, the Ministry of Munitions was staffed at the top levels by businessmen, recruited by Lloyd George and loaned by their companies for the length of the war. These men were able to coordinate the needs of big business with those of the state and reach a compromise on price and profit that was acceptable to both sides. In addition, government agents bought essential supplies from abroad. Once bought, their distribution had to be controlled in order to prevent speculative price rises and to enable normal marketing to continue. The whole of the Indian jute crop, for example, was bought and distributed in this way. Steel, wool, leather and flax soon came under similar controls.

Coal

The supply of coal was essential to the maintenance of Britain's industry and so to the war effort. Yet this supply was compromised in the early days of the war by the vast numbers of miners who volunteered for the armed forces. Production fell and prices soared. The situation in the South Wales coalfield was additionally complicated by a bitter coal strike in July 1915. Various proposals for State control of the coal mines were stalled by the government, partly because the Liberal Party was heavily dependent on contributions from coal owners to its party funds. However, by the beginning of December 1916, DORA had been extended to cover the South Wales mines and a coal controller appointed in February 1917. Mines remained in private ownership throughout the war, but their profits were fixed at 1913 levels and pay negotiation on national, rather than local, levels was permitted. Any surplus profits went to the Treasury, where they were kept and used to make up any falling profits in individual mines to the 1913 level.

Food

For most of the war, most of the people of Britain had enough to eat. There may not have been choice and there were certainly shortages, but no one faced starvation. Intensified submarine warfare in the autumn of 1916 stopped necessary supplies getting through to Britain and shortages became serious the following spring. Not only had the civilian population to be fed, but so had the armed forces abroad. By April, Britain had only four days' supply of sugar and nine weeks' supply of wheat left. People hoarded food and prices rocketed. Lloyd George acted. He appointed

- Lord Devonport to be food controller with responsibility for the distribution of food
- Sir George Prothero to be President of the Board of Agriculture, with the specific responsibility of increasing domestic food production.

Was food distributed fairly? Lord Devonport proved to be useless. He spent his time at the new Ministry of Food dealing with minutiae. He issued prohibitions against sugar icing and restrictions on window displays of luxury foodstuffs and the kind of food that could be eaten in tea shops. As prices rose, Devonport issued appeals for voluntary rationing to be supervised by local food committees; appeals to the people to save grain were read from pulpits every Sunday; and he instituted 'meatless days'. These measures had no real impact. Appointed in December 1916, he resigned in May 1917.

Devonport was replaced by Lord Rhondda, who was effective from the start. He established a system of rationing for essential foodstuffs by setting up statutory food control committees throughout the country, each area with a food office that issued registration cards. There was plenty of opportunity for different sorts of local initiatives and Birmingham, for example, went ahead with its own scheme. Bacon, butter, margarine, meat, sugar and tea were among the essential foodstuffs to be rationed. Bread was never rationed and the biggest grievance people had with it was its expense. In the spring of 1917, bread cost 1 shilling for a 4lb loaf, twice its 1914 price. Lord Rhondda persuaded the government to subsidise the cost of bread and the price of a 4lb loaf was fixed at 9d. From November, there was a subsidy on potatoes.

Was domestic food production increased? George Prothero set up a system of local agricultural committees that were very successful. By 1918, 3 million additional acres had been taken into cultivation: 1 million tons more of wheat and 1.3 million tons more of potatoes were produced.

Drink

In the years before 1914, all establishments selling alcohol had to be licensed and had a set closing time. There was some regional variation but, in general, pubs were open for most of the day. Opening times of 6.00am until midnight were common. On the outbreak of war, both the War Office and the Admiralty reported servicemen appearing either drunk on duty or with heavy hangovers. One of the earliest DORA regulations was to limit the opening hours of pubs close to harbours. This developed into a widespread campaign on the part of the government to limit the incidence of drunkenness among the civilian population. Their justification for doing this was that, quite simply, drunkenness kept people away from the workplace and lost thousands of hours of production that the country couldn't afford.

- The chief officer of police in any licensing district could restrict the hours during which alcohol could be sold.
- A central control board was set up to control alcohol licensing in areas where excessive drunkenness was judged to be impeding the war effort. It set up canteen

facilities in new munitions areas and supported the concept of 'model pubs'.

- Other governmental attacks on heavy drinking included increasing prices, decreasing the alcoholic content of beer and restricting the sale of spirits. Throughout the war, budgets put heavier and heavier taxation on spirits.

These measures were very effective. In 1914, the average weekly conviction rate for drunkenness in England and Wales was 3388; by the end of 1918, this had fallen to 449. In Scotland, the figures were 1485 and 355. Public drunkenness declined as a feature of the British social scene.

HOW WAS TRANSPORT CONTROLLED?

It was clearly essential at a time of total war to be able to move troops and civilians, raw materials and manufactured goods quickly and efficiently to where they were needed, both within Britain and overseas.

Railways
The necessity of government control of the railways had been recognised as early as 1871, when the Regulation of Forces Act stated that in time of war the railways were to be placed at the disposal of the government. So, in August 1914, the railways passed easily into the control of government's Railway Executive Committee. In reality, however, they were run by the managers of the main railway companies. This arrangement worked well: profits were kept at 1913 levels and the government, in return for free transport of troops, made up any deficits.

Shipping
The merchant marine was as essential to survival in total war as the Royal Navy, yet by December 1916 fewer than half of Britain's merchant ships and none of its great passenger liners had been requisitioned by the government. This was all changed by the appointment of Sir John Maclay, a Scottish shipowner, as shipping controller working in conjunction with a committee of management comprising all significant British shipowners. In May 1917, Eric Geddes, as controller of the navy, headed a

separate department. By 1918, almost all merchant shipping had been requisitioned by the Ministry of Shipping.

A Canal Control Committee, set up in March 1917, was responsible for all inland waterways not owned and run by railway companies.

WHAT DID IT ALL COST?

Paying for the war: in cash terms
It cost the government roughly £3.85 million a day to keep the war going. Where did the money come from?

- Increasing the **national debt** from £625 million in 1914 to £7980 million in 1918 met about 70 per cent of the total expenditure.
- The remaining 30 per cent was made up from taxation, and successive chancellors of the Exchequer steadily raised revenue in this way:
  - Lloyd George (1914–15) increased the standard rate of income tax from 9d in the pound to 1s 6d in the pound.
  - McKenna (1915–16) raised income tax to 3s 6d in the pound and introduced a tax on excess profits.
  - Bonar Law (1916–18) raised income tax to 6s in the pound and excess profits tax to 80 per cent
  In 1914, 1.5 million people paid income tax; by 1918, the number had risen to 7.75 million.
- The government persuaded people to buy war bonds. These were, in effect, loans from individuals and institutions to the government that were to be paid back at the end of the war, plus interest. This formed part of the national debt but, for the individuals concerned, it was a form of saving.
- The banks stopped issuing gold in exchange for bank notes. The gold was kept in reserve for a government emergency – and, overall, more bank notes were printed than there was gold to back them.

Paying for the war: in human terms
The mobilisation of a volunteer and then conscript army, together with spasmodic raids on coastal towns, meant that

there was hardly a family in the land untouched by tragedy. Herbert Asquith lost one son and Andrew Bonar Law, two. Neither politician completely recovered from his loss. Nearly 750,000 British servicemen were killed. Thousands more were injured: of these over 240,000 had leg or arm amputations. Most of those who died, or who were hurt mentally and physically, were young men aged between 18 and 25. These were the 'lost generation' and losing them meant that tens of thousands of children grew up fatherless; widows grew old alone; and young women never married and remained childless all their lives. The world lost a huge range of potential talent. The cost in human terms was incalculable.

WHAT DID THE WAR CHANGE?

The experience of total war was so cataclysmic that ideas and attitudes of the people who lived through it were bound to undergo change, as were institutions and organisations.

Why had the power of the trade unions increased?

The war created a huge demand for additional industrial workers who were absolutely essential to the war effort. This gave the trade unions tremendous bargaining power and they exercised this, in the main, through their **Trades Union Congress**. Government ministers tried to gain union support over banning strikes, restrictive practices, and accepting dilution and conscription (see pages 80–2) and, to a large extent, they succeeded. This cooperation and closeness had two main effects:

- Trade unions came to be seen as a responsible, integral part of the country's political life.
- Workers in some industries distrusted the bonds being forged between government and the Trades Union Congress, and felt that not enough was being done for them. In various parts of the country, **shop stewards** acted in defiance of full-time officials. One such area was 'Red Clydeside', where there were violent protests at union abandonment of the right to strike when the TUC agreed to support the Munitions Act. Shop

(see pages 80–2)

KEY ORGANISATION

Trades Union Congress
An umbrella organisation of the trade union movement, by 1900 the TUC represented just over 1 million workers and supported the setting up of the Labour Representation Committee. One of the aims of the LRC was to bring trade union issues to the attention of Parliament and to elect its own MPs. In 1906, the 29 LRC MPs became the basis of the new Labour Party with which the TUC maintained strong links. By 1914, the TUC had 2.5 million members.

KEY ROLE

Shop steward A union member appointed by fellow workers on the shop-floor to represent them to the union. Shop stewards usually worked with the full-time union officials, appointed by the union headquarters, representing the union to the workers and the workers to the union. There were occasions when the needs and demands of the shop-floor workers and their shop stewards did not coincide with the aims of the union hierarchy.

Year	Working days lost	Number of strikes	Number of strikers	Strike activity, 1913–19
1913	9,804,000	1459	664,000	
1914	9,878,000	972	447,000	
1915	2,953,000	672	448,000	
1916	2,446,000	532	276,000	
1917	5,647,000	730	872,000	
1918	5,875,000	1165	1,116,000	
1919	34,969,000	1352	2,591,000	

stewards were also instrumental in the strikes in the engineering industry in May 1917.

Trade union membership grew from 4 million in 1914 to over 6 million by the time the war ended in 1918. During this time, many industrial workers benefited from higher wages and improved working conditions. But, despite the presence of Labour Party ministers in government, this didn't mean industrial peace. It seemed in many ways that, as the leadership of the trade union movement moved closer to the government, it lost the support of its ordinary, working-class membership.

Lloyd George was so disturbed by the increase in strikes that he appointed commissions to investigate the causes of industrial unrest. They found that these were the rising cost of living, dilution, conscription, profiteering and administrative incompetence. There is evidence, too, that many industrial workers believed that the burdens of war were falling too heavily on the working classes, both at home and in the armed forces. Many of these workers were enfranchised for the first time in 1918, giving them political power for the first time.

How had the role and status of women changed?

The war undoubtedly had an impact on the role and status of women, but one that is difficult to quantify. Clearly (see pages 55–7) it was one of the driving factors in granting women the right to vote, but, ironically, the women who were given the vote in 1918 were not those young women who had risked their lives in munitions factories. But the war had brought about other, more subtle changes.

- The 1919 Sex Disqualification Act opened jury service, the magistracy and the legal profession to women and gave them limited access to high-level posts in the civil service.
- The 1919 State Register of Nurses recognised nursing as a profession.
- The National Insurance Acts of 1918, 1920 and 1921 made women eligible for national insurance benefits.

BUT

The increased job opportunities for women provided by the war were short-lived. In 1914, 5.96 million women were in paid employment; by 1918, this had risen to 7.31 million. However, a year later, the figure had dropped to almost the 1914 level. While it is true that many women returned to 'hearth and home', giving up their work to the returning men, it is also true that the postwar slump cut job opportunities anyway. There were changes in the variety of work women were perceived as capable of undertaking, with engineering and commerce overtaking domestic service, and in the 1930s there was again a steady growth of women in paid employment.

Did people's attitudes and behaviour change?

Closely linked to the changing perceptions of the role and status of women were changing perceptions of the sort of social behaviour society found acceptable.

- Relationships between the sexes became more open (chaperones were unheard of after the war) and more personal freedoms existed. In February 1918, the National Council for the Unmarried Mother and her Child was founded, and the work of Marie Stopes made contraception more widely available.
- Men and women smoked more, and smoked more openly in public; swearing became socially acceptable.
- Women's increasing financial independence was reflected in shorter, more practical haircuts, shorter hemlines and the wearing of trousers – usually called 'slacks'.
- Theatres and music halls put on reviews and romantic plays that appealed to young women as well as young men, and it became (just) acceptable for women to go alone into the more respectable public houses.

Did the war affect the class structure of British society?

In crude terms, the nature of a class system can be determined by the distribution of wealth within a country. In Britain, the distribution of wealth before and after the First World War was only slightly altered.

- In 1914, 0.4 per cent of the population owned 66 per cent of the country's wealth; by 1929, 2.5 per cent owned the same proportion.
- There was, however, a significant rise in salaried workers as opposed to those paid an hourly rate. In 1911, 1.7 million people received salaries, about 12 per cent of the working population. This had risen to 22 per cent, about 2.7 million people, by 1921. This was because of a general increase in managerial work or white-collar work and the expansion of the professions.
- There was a corresponding decline – about 30 per cent – in the number of domestic servants employed after the war.
- At the bottom end of the social scale, it is reasonably safe to say that, for the working class in general, wage increases usually, but not always, kept ahead of price increases.

It seems clear that the First World War, insofar as relationships between government and governed were concerned, accelerated processes that began before 1914. The state was taking an increasingly interventionist role in the lives of its citizens – citizens who were becoming increasingly independent and unwilling to accept the standards and values of prewar society.

SUMMARY QUESTIONS

1 What is 'total war'? What were the implications of total war for Britain's civilian population?

2 Why might Liberals have problems with what the government was doing on the Home Front?

3 What, in your judgement, was the most important change brought about by the First World War?

CHAPTER 9

The Irish question: Home Rule or partition?

The relationship between the island of Ireland and mainland Britain has always been a tricky one. It is a relationship dominated by fear and mistrust, anger and guilt, prejudice and arrogance. How did this come about?

A TROUBLESOME COLONY?

In the sixteenth and seventeenth centuries, various British governments deliberately settled Protestants in a predominantly Catholic Ireland. The Protestants were, in general, given land and positions over and above the indigenous Catholics with the aim of keeping Ireland peaceful, subdued and no threat to mainland Britain. It didn't quite work out like that. Discrimination against Catholics – political, legal and economic – created a legacy of bitterness that boiled over into violence when various flash-points in the troubled relationship were reached. Many in Ireland resented being treated, in their view, as a British colonial possession. And in many ways, this was the British attitude to Ireland.

The 1801 Act of Union enabled Ireland to send 100 MPs and sixteen peers to Westminster, but it simultaneously removed the Irish legislature. Ireland was still ruled by a viceroy based in Dublin Castle and a chief secretary with a seat in the Cabinet. Britain provided the police force – the Royal Irish Constabulary – and, when trouble threatened, never hesitated to send in the British army as it did in 1916, 1919 and 1921. Some politicians attempted to improve the lot of the Irish peasant, for example by way of the 1881 Land Commission. But this could be seen as the act of a colonial power, and, indeed, one of the Conservative Party's arguments against Home Rule was that it would herald the break-up of the British Empire.

GLADSTONE'S ATTEMPTS AT BRINGING HOME RULE TO IRELAND

William Gladstone, the leader of the Liberal Party, took up the cause of Home Rule for Ireland sometime in the summer of 1885. We are not sure if this was a genuine conversion or if it was a conversion based on political calculation rather than principle. Gladstone certainly needed support from the **Irish Nationalist Party** if the Liberals were to get back into power, and he got it. In the general election later that year, Gladstone's Liberals were back in government, with a majority of 86 over the Conservatives. This was exactly the number of Irish Nationalist MPs, who thus held the **balance of power**.

Gladstone's first Home Rule Bill 1886 allowed only limited independence for Ireland: the British government was to retain control of security, foreign policy and financial institutions. **Parnell** and the Irish Nationalist Party saw it as a final settlement of the Irish question, but the **Unionists** regarded it as a total betrayal of the Act of Union. Randolph Churchill, Winston's father, warned Gladstone that he would 'agitate Ulster, even beyond constitutional means'.

True to his word, in 1886 he travelled Ireland to rally opposition to the bill. Part of a letter from Randolph Churchill to a Liberal Unionist made his views clear:

> *If political parties and political leaders should be so lost to every feeling of honour and courage as to hand over, for the sake of purchasing a short parliamentary peace, the lives and liberties of the Loyalists of Ireland to their hereditary and most bitter foes, make no doubt on this point – Ulster will not be a consenting party. Ulster will fight, Ulster will be right.*

Randolph Churchill almost exactly caught the mood of Unionists in Ireland. Already there was drilling and marching, oath taking and the buying and collecting of guns in order to defend the union. Later in the year, riots broke out in Belfast and 32 people were killed. Gladstone's bill divided the Liberal Party and failed to get through the

Charles Stuart Parnell (1846–91) Born into an Anglo-Irish Protestant family, he became MP for Meath in 1875. In 1877, he was chosen as president of the Home Rule Confederation of Great Britain. In 1880, he became leader of the Irish Nationalist Party in Parliament and president of the Irish Land League, which hoped to prevent a repetition of the famine of the 1840s by reforming the landlord–tenant system. In the years 1880–1 he organised agitation in the Irish countryside and successfully pressurised the Liberal government into giving tenants greater protection. Believing firmly in Irish independence, he turned the Irish Nationalist Party into a disciplined political party that was the driving force behind Gladstone's Home Rule Bill of 1886. Parnell's position was damaged by false accusations that he was linked to Fenian violence and by being named as a co-respondent in a divorce case. Deserted by the non-conformist Liberals and the Catholic Irish because of this, he was forced to resign as leader of the Irish Nationalist Party and died in 1891, aged 45.

KEY GROUP

Unionists Those people who supported the Act of Union of Britain with Ireland.

Commons, though Parnell was encouraged in that the bill had, for the first time, recognised the ability of the people of Ireland to govern themselves. Gladstone resigned and, in the general election that followed, the Conservative–Liberal Unionists won 393 seats, while Gladstonian Liberals managed a total of 191 MPs. This put Home Rule on hold for six years.

Gladstone's second Home Rule Bill 1893 was slightly more successful than the first. In 1892, the Liberals were back in power, but it was a power where, again, the Irish Nationalists held the balance. The Gladstonian Liberals gained 80 seats, giving them a total of 272 MPs. The Conservatives and Liberal Unionists won 313 seats – and the Irish Nationalist Party, despite having been split by Parnell, returned a key 81 MPs. This time, Gladstone's Home Rule Bill got through the Commons without any real problems, but was heavily defeated in the Lords by 419 votes to 41. The House of Lords had an in-built Conservative–Unionist majority and there was no chance that it would agree to Home Rule for Ireland. Nevertheless, the very fact that a major political party was prepared to back Home Rule for Ireland hardened attitudes among Unionists and led to the emergence of very well-organised support for the Union.

KEY PLACE

Ulster Originally, this referred to the historical northern province of Ireland, comprising the counties of Antrim, Armagh, Cavan, Down, Donegal, Fermanagh, Londonderry, Monaghan and Tyrone. After 1922, Cavan, Donegal and Monaghan were left out of what was then defined as Ulster.

The growth of Unionism affected the whole of Ireland. Unionism wasn't confined to Ulster alone. In the 1890s, there were about 250,000 Unionists in southern Ireland who were usually land-owning Protestants and who were important, not for their numbers (which were small) but for the credibility they gave to leading Unionists' claim that the desire to remain united with Britain wasn't confined to Ulster alone. The growth of Unionism had religious, political and economic effects:

- In the 1861 census, 78 per cent of the population of Ireland was Catholic. This had risen to 81 per cent by 1911. In Ulster, however, Protestants remained in the majority. The emergence of a Home Rule movement forced the two prominent Protestant groups – Presbyterians and Anglicans – into an alliance in which religious, political and economic differences were submerged into the slogan 'Home Rule means Rome Rule'.

- The **Orange Order** was revived and became a focal point for Protestant Unionist disaffection and for agitation against Home Rule.
- Growing demands for Home Rule meant that, between 1885 and 1910 in Ireland, Liberal Party candidates lost votes to Unionists if they wanted to maintain the Union and to the Irish Nationalist Party if they wanted Home Rule. However, Unionism became increasingly associated with Ulster because it was there that Unionists had most support. The first moves were made to set up a formal Unionist party.
- There were profound economic differences between Ulster and the rest of Ireland. In the 1890s, Ireland was predominantly an agricultural country – with the exception of Ulster. Ulster was industrialised and was dependent upon Britain for markets and raw materials. Yet another reason for Ulster to oppose Home Rule.

THE LIBERALS TRY AGAIN IN 1912

When the Liberals swept to electoral victory in 1906, the size of their majority meant that they could carry almost any legislation they chose through the Commons. The Liberal leadership chose to take the Irish question slowly. While the party could depend upon getting Home Rule through the Commons, the House of Lords, with its built-in Unionist majority, was a different matter. The government therefore focused on the legislation that could pass through the Lords without too much difficulty, and so Home Rule for Ireland slipped down the political agenda.

In 1910, everything changed. The Parliament Act (see page 34) meant that the Lords could only delay legislation; they couldn't reject it for ever. Home Rule was back on the agenda. After the second election of 1910, the Irish Nationalist Party held the balance of power, just as it had done in 1886 and 1893. The Liberals needed the support of the Irish National Party to push the Parliament Act through the Commons. They got it – and the price was an

The Orange Order The aim and purpose of the Orange Order, founded in 1795, was to defend Protestant interests against Catholics. It aimed, too, to celebrate the memory of William of Orange who had defeated the Catholic King of England, James II, at the Battle of the Boyne in 1690.

HEINEMANN ADVANCED HISTORY

Irish Home Rule Bill. But this time many Liberals genuinely wanted Home Rule for Ireland.

The third Home Rule Bill 1912 was basically the same as that of 1893:

- The Westminster Parliament was supreme and responsible for decisions on matters of foreign policy, trade, customs and excise, and military affairs.
- There was to be an Irish Parliament with two chambers – a small senate and a larger elected commons.
- Ireland was to send 42 MPs to Westminster.

What was important about this bill was that, despite the growing force of Ulster Unionism, it applied to the whole of Ireland. Ulster was not excluded and there was no intention to do so, despite Unionists' insistence that they would resist Home Rule by whatever means possible. The bill passed the Commons by January 1913, despite fierce opposition from Conservatives and Unionists. A fortnight later it was rejected by the Lords, but this was no longer a problem. They could only delay the bill. It would become law in 1914.

The Ulster Unionists, backed by the Conservative Party, were in no mood to accept Home Rule for Ireland. The delay between the rejection of the bill by the Lords and it automatically becoming law gave both the Unionists and the Irish Nationalists time to mobilise.

RESISTANCE IN ULSTER

Resistance in Ulster to Home Rule began as soon as the Parliament Act became law and Home Rule for the whole of Ireland became more than likely. This Unionist resistance was coordinated by **Edward Carson**, the leader of the Irish Unionist Parliamentary Party and James Craig, leader of the Ulster Unionist Council. Inevitably, it was countered by similarly organised Irish nationalist forces determined to obtain Home Rule.

KEY PERSON

**Edward Carson
(1854–1935)** A southern Ireland Protestant, he became a successful Dublin lawyer and Unionist politician. In 1892, he moved his practice to London and became a successful lawyer. He was Solicitor-General (1900–5) for Ireland and Britain and a leading figure in the Tory party. In 1910, he was elected leader of the Unionist Party and spearheaded resistance to the third Home Rule Bill, believing that the whole of Ireland should remain under British rule. However, by 1914 he had reluctantly accepted the necessity of partition. In 1915, he became Attorney-General, and played a major role in removing Asquith from office in 1916. As First Lord of the Admiralty (1916–17) he proved to be a poor administrator but remained a member of the war cabinet until 1918. After 1918, he was less active in Irish politics and resigned as leader in 1921 before Northern Ireland was established. He became a law lord in that year after turning down the post of prime minister of Northern Ireland.

- In September 1911, James Craig organised a mass meeting that was attended by about 50,000 people, mainly Unionists from Orange lodges and other similar organisations throughout Ulster. This was a rallying call.
- A year of meetings, conferences, letters and petitions culminated in 'Covenant Day' on 28 September 1912, when 250,000 people signed, sometimes in their own blood, a solemn league and covenant drawn up by Edward Carson:

> *Being convinced that Home Rule would be disastrous to the material well-being of Ulster as well as of the whole of Ireland, subversive of our civil and religious freedom, destructive of our citizenship and perilous to the unity of the empire, we men of Ulster, loyal subjects of his Gracious Majesty King George V, do hereby pledge ourselves in solemn covenant to stand by one another in defending for ourselves and our children our cherished position of equal citizenship in the United Kingdom, and using all means to defeat the present conspiracy to set up a Home Rule Parliament in Ireland. And in the event of such a Parliament being forced upon us, we further solemnly and mutually pledge ourselves to refuse to recognise its authority. God save the King.*

- In January 1913, the Ulster Volunteer Force (UVF), an armed paramilitary organisation, was set up. It had officers who had had experience of serving in the British army. By March 1914, it had 100,000 members.

Edward Carson at an anti-Home Rule demonstration, September 1912

John Redmond (1856–1918) Born into a Catholic merchant family in county Wexford, he became clerk to the House of Commons in 1880 and an Irish Parliamentary Party MP. He was MP for New Ross (1880–5), North Wexford (1885–91) and Waterford City (1891–1918) A firm believer in Home Rule, he became leader of the Irish Party in 1900 and grew in power and importance after the general elections of 1910 when he was able to push the Liberals into introducing a Home Rule bill. However, when Tory opposition mounted, he looked increasingly weak and dependent on the Liberal alliance. On the outbreak of war in 1914, he supported the war effort but after the Easter Rising the Irish Party was defeated in several by-elections by Sinn Féin. Redmond died in 1918, just before the final defeat of his party in the 1918 elections.

- Nationalists in the south of Ireland responded by setting up the Irish Volunteers, a similar paramilitary organisation but pledged to support Home Rule. **John Redmond**, leader of the Irish Nationalist Party, controlled the Irish Volunteers.

How did the Conservative Party react?

The Conservative Party had linked itself firmly to the Unionist cause, but would it go as far as supporting armed insurrection against the will of the British Parliament if the Home Rule bill become law? In July 1912, the Conservative leader, Andrew Bonar Law, attended a mass meeting of Unionists at Blenheim Palace, where he shared the platform with Edward Carson and declared:

> *We shall not be guided by the considerations or bound by the restraints which would influence us in an ordinary constitutional struggle. If an attempt were made to deprive these men of their birthright, they would be justified in resisting such an attempt by all means in their power, including force. I can imagine no length of resistance to which Ulster can go in which I would not be prepared to support them.*

There were several reasons why the Conservatives were so unenthusiastic at this time about Home Rule:

- They had been out of office since 1905 and believed that opposition to Home Rule would make them popular with the electorate.
- They maintained that the Liberals didn't have a mandate to introduce Home Rule because the second 1910 election did not gain them any more seats than they had had in the first election of that year.
- They believed that the Liberals were being 'jumped' into Home Rule because they needed the support of the Irish Nationalists for the Parliament Act.
- They opposed the attitudes and policies of the Liberal government, which they saw as an attack on the Empire and on property.

How did the Liberal government react?

The 1912 Home Rule bill, like the two previous Liberal bills, did not separate Ulster from the rest of Ireland. Home Rule was for the island of Ireland. In the delay before the Home Rule bill became law, there was increasing pressure on the government from Unionists to make Ulster a special case. There was, in other words, pressure for Ulster to be partitioned from the rest of Ireland. There was equal pressure from the Irish Nationalists for the government to keep Ireland whole and not even consider partition.

So what happened?

* The government worked frantically behind the scenes to bring about a compromise that would be acceptable to both sides. Several times the Liberal government nearly broke apart under the strain of the crisis.
* There was considerable Liberal sympathy for the Ulster Protestants and their plea that they be allowed their religious rights and liberties.
* Gradually, the view grew that Ulster had to be offered a separate deal and this was accepted by Asquith, Lloyd George and Churchill.
* But to agree to partition would end Liberal support from the Irish Nationalists, on whose vote the government depended, and would eventually mean a government defeat and a Conservative victory at the subsequent elections.
* Eventually, Asquith persuaded John Redmond and the Irish Nationalists to agree that any Irish county could opt out of Home Rule at any time during the first six years of Home Rule.
* Edward Carson's Unionist support prevented him from compromising.
* King George V invited all sides to meet at a constitutional conference in July 1914.

WHAT WAS THE SITUATION IN AUGUST 1914?

By August 1914, Ireland was on the brink of civil war:

- British army officers stationed in Ireland made it clear that they would not, if ordered, take action against the paramilitary Protestant UVF.
- The UVF had successfully smuggled into Ireland, mostly from Germany, around 20,000 rifles and 3 million rounds of ammunition. The police and military had been physically prevented from interfering and made no attempt, then or later, to enforce the law.
- In southern Ireland, the pro-Home Rule Irish Volunteers had been smuggling arms too, but in July 1914 police and the army attempted to seize a shipload that was being off-loaded. They were beaten off but returned later with reinforcements, killing three civilians and injuring more than 30 unarmed civilians.
- There was consensus in the government and among moderate Nationalists that some sort of special case would have to be made for Ulster.
- Edward Carson had accepted the inevitability of some form of Home Rule for part of Ireland. Originally wanting to kill Home Rule altogether, he now demanded that just six of the nine Ulster counties should be allowed to remain with Britain.

On 4 August 1914, Britain declared war on Germany. The Home Rule bill, affecting the whole of Ireland and making no concessions to Ulster, became law on 18 September 1914, and the government promptly suspended it until the war ended.

Did Irish Catholics and Protestants fight with Britain in the 1914–18 war?

Many German and American observers believed that, because of the situation in Ireland, Britain would not be able to fight at all. They thought that all Britain's resources would be needed to crush rebellion in Ireland, and they were wrong. As soon as war was declared, Britain was assured of Irish support.

- Before the end of 1915, over 29,000 men from Edward

Carson's UVF had volunteered to fight and separate units were formed from the UVF itself.

- About 80,000 of John Redmond's Irish Nationalists served with the British army, changing their name to the National Volunteers. On 25 September 1914, John Redmond declared:

> *I have come here tonight to join with the responses of all parties, and all creeds and all classes in Ireland to tell the Prime Minister and the people of Great Britain that Ireland is in full and heartfelt sympathy with the objects of this war. And that she will bear her share of the burdens and sufferings entailed by that war. Ireland's right to autonomy has been conceded by the democracy of Great Britain, and therefore Ireland will feel bound in honour to take her place side by side with all the other autonomous portions of the King's dominions in upholding her interests.*

However, not all Irish Nationalists felt the same, and the change of name marked a split in the Home Rule movement. The more extreme elements of the Irish Nationalist movement retained the name 'Irish Nationalist' and, led by Padraic Pearse and Eoin MacNeill, refused to fight in a war they believed had nothing to do with them. Britain's cause was not, they maintained, their cause. The defeats in the first year of the war and horrendous losses persuaded more and more people to join with Pearse and MacNeill in refusing to volunteer to fight. Their attitude is summed up by James Connolly, who was later (see pages 103–4) one of the leaders of the Easter Rising of 1916.

> *We have no foreign enemy except the treacherous government of England – a government that even whilst it is calling upon us to die for it, refuses to give a straight answer to our demand for Home Rule.*

THE EASTER RISING, APRIL 1916

The extreme Irish Nationalists formed the Irish Republican Brotherhood, and they planned armed insurrection against the hated British.

Their leaders were:

- Roger Casement, a former member of the British consular service, and a firm supporter of Irish nationalism
- James Connolly, born in Edinburgh of Irish parents, a strong believer in socialism and Ireland's claim to nationhood, who attempted to create, in his Citizen's Army, an efficient fighting force
- Padraic Pearse, a schoolteacher with a romantic view of Irish history and a belief in the cleansing quality of warfare
- **Eamonn de Valera**, born in New York but brought up in rural Ireland, a mathematics teacher.

From the start, the Easter Rising was marked by dissent and disarray.

- Eoin MacNeill, chief of staff of the Irish Volunteers, took the view that he would only support an armed insurrection if it stood a good chance of being successful. Anxious for his support, and the support of the Irish Volunteers, the Military Council of the Irish Republican Brotherhood deceived him into believing, by way of a forged letter, that the British were going to disarm the Volunteers. Fearful of seeing his Irish Volunteers disarmed, MacNeill agreed to support the rising. On discovering the deception, a furious MacNeill sent out orders countermanding the rising.
- A German shipment of arms lay at the bottom of Queenstown harbour. The submarine *Aud* had been intercepted by the Royal Navy, and had been scuttled by her captain.
- Roger Casement had been in Germany trying to recruit Irish prisoners-of-war for an armed rising against the British. Disillusioned by the lack of support, a German submarine landed him back home in southern Ireland on the Kerry coast. He was going to advise against the rising, but was arrested on the beach.

None of this, however, deterred the militant Irish Republican Brotherhood. Their detailed preparations for an uprising on Easter Monday involved seizure of chosen

KEY PERSON

Eamonn de Valera (1882–1975) He was brought up in Ireland by relatives after his father's death and mother's remarriage. Originally a mathematics teacher, he joined the Irish Volunteers in 1913 and commanded a battalion during the Easter Rising of 1916. He was sentenced to death, but his sentence was commuted to imprisonment and he was released in 1917 when he was elected Sinn Féin MP for Clare. He broke with hard-line Republicans in 1926 (who kept the name Sinn Féin) and formed his own Fianna Fail Party, entering the Dail in 1927. After winning the 1932 election, he became Taoisearch for sixteen years, during which time he promoted Irish independence by establishing a new constitution that virtually undid the treaty settlement. It embodied Catholic values, banning contraception and divorce, and introducing a rigid form of literary censorship. In the Second World War, he officially followed a strictly neutralist policy. In fact, he engaged in low-profile co-operation with the British government. He lost office in 1948, but returned as Taoisearch in 1951–4 and 1957–9. He was president of Ireland from 1959 until his retirement, aged 90, in 1973.

strongpoints in Dublin. The hope was that this would incite rebellion in the rest of Ireland. A forlorn hope, in view of MacNeill's instructions.

The rising began on Easter Monday 1916 and took the authorities by surprise. This gave the rebels an advantage and they were quickly able to establish themselves in their chosen strongpoints, including the General Post Office which became the centre of operations. It was from there that Padraic Pearse proclaimed an independent Irish republic:

> We declare the right of the people of Ireland to the ownership of Ireland, and to the unfettered control of Irish destinies, to be sovereign and indefeasible. The long usurpation of that right by a foreign people and government has not extinguished that right, nor can it ever be extinguished except by the destruction of the Irish people. Standing on that fundamental right we hereby proclaim the Irish republic as a sovereign independent state, and we pledge our lives and the lives of our comrades-in-arms to the cause of its freedom, of its welfare, and of its exaltation among the nations.

The rebellion didn't last long. Street fighting in Dublin lasted for about a week, a week in which about 1600 rebels faced 12,000 British troops and a gunboat. The outcome was never really in doubt: on Sunday 30 April, Connolly and Pearce ordered an unconditional surrender. Four hundred and fifty Irish people had been killed and 2614 injured; 116 British soldiers died and 368 were wounded.

How did the British in Ireland react?

The British troops and police in Ireland acted with a force that many considered inappropriately heavy and vindictive:

- British artillery pounded Dublin and many beautiful buildings, for example in Sackville Street, were almost completely destroyed.
- The British commander, General Maxwell, took 3430 men and 79 women into custody. Many were released after interrogation, but 1841 were taken to Britain and interned. Ninety people were sentenced to death although in the end only fifteen were executed.

Those who were executed were regarded as martyrs in the cause of Irish nationalism, and the aftermath of the Easter Rising created an enormous surge of popular sympathy.

Did the British government's policy towards Ireland change after the Easter Rising?

After the Easter Rising, British policy became a curious mixture of conciliation and threat:

- Herbert Asquith, the Liberal Prime Minister, stopped the shooting of prisoners. Acknowledging that law and order had broken down, he decided that negotiations for Home Rule should go ahead and be implemented before the end of the war.
- David Lloyd George was sent to Dublin in May to start negotiations, in the hope that his negotiating skills would find a settlement on which both Edward Carson and John Redmond could agree. Lloyd George found one: he promised Redmond that the exclusion of Ulster from Home Rule for the whole of Ireland would be only temporary; he promised Carson that it would be permanent.
- An Irish Convention was summoned for July 1917, but by then attitudes had hardened. Most of the Republican groups had combined under Sinn Féin and refused to attend, and the Ulster Unionists would not move from their position regarding the need to treat Ulster separately.
- Lloyd George decided to extend conscription to Ireland. He made it clear he would offer Home Rule in exchange. Although this remained a threat only, it united opposition to the British government as nothing else could have done. Irish Nationalists withdrew from the House of Commons and joined with Sinn Féin in urging the Irish people to resist conscription. The Irish Catholic bishops joined in, persuading the Irish people to resist conscription 'by every means consonant with the law of God'.
- The 'conscription issue' posed such a security problem in Northern Ireland that, far from raising desperately needed recruits, 87,500 British troops had to be stationed in Ireland to keep the peace.

De Valera becomes a national leader

Eamonn De Valera was sentenced to death after the Easter Rising, but the sentence wasn't carried out because of the intervention of the American consul in Dublin. In the summer of 1916, he was released from prison and began campaigning for Home Rule:

- At a by-election in East Clare in the summer of 1917, he was elected MP.
- In October 1917, he became president of Sinn Féin.
- In December 1917, he became president of the Irish Volunteers.

By 1918, Eamonn De Valera was an Irish national leader and Sinn Féin a strong republican organisation. Here, De Valera sets out his demands on his election as president of Sinn Féin:

> *This organisation of Sinn Féin aims at securing international recognition of Ireland as an independent Irish Republic. Some of us would wish to have a republican form of government. Some might prefer other forms of government. But we are all united on this: that we want complete and absolute independence. I only wish to say that there is no thought of having a monarchy in which the monarch would be of the House of Windsor.*

THE GENERAL ELECTION OF 1918

The Irish vote in the general election of 1918 showed a marked swing to Sinn Féin, as the table shows. Sinn Féin members refused to take up their Westminster seats, and set up their own Dáil Éireann (Irish Parliament) in Dublin. The only Irish representation in the House of Commons was that of MPs with decidedly Unionist leanings.

Irish MPs	Before 1918 election	After 1918 election
Irish Nationalist	68	6
Independent	10	0
Unionist	18	26
Sinn Féin	7	73

Swing to Sinn Féin, 1918

THE GOVERNMENT OF IRELAND ACT 1920

The Dáil Éireann was committed to achieving an Irish republic and it began by simply not cooperating with the British administration in Ireland. By the end of 1919, Lloyd George had proposed another 'solution': the Government of Ireland Act. It proposed:

- separate parliaments in Dublin and Belfast, with 28 and 52 seats respectively – Ireland was to be partitioned
- Ulster, with a parliament in Belfast, to comprise the counties of Antrim, Armagh, Derry, Down, Fermanagh and Tyrone
- 42 Irish members to continue to sit as MPs at Westminster
- the British government to retain control over war and peace, foreign affairs, customs and excise, law and order, the armed forces and land and agricultural policy
- a Council of Ireland, comprising 20 members from Dublin and 20 from Belfast.

THE KINDEST CUT OF ALL.

WELSH WIZARD. "I NOW PROCEED TO CUT THIS MAP INTO TWO PARTS AND PLACE THEM IN THE HAT. AFTER A SUITABLE INTERVAL THEY WILL BE FOUND TO HAVE COME TOGETHER OF THEIR OWN ACCORD—(ASIDE)—AT LEAST LET'S HOPE SO; I'VE NEVER DONE THIS TRICK BEFORE."

Punch cartoon of 1920 on the partition of Ireland, 'The kindest cut of all'

The Bill was dismissed by Sinn Féin, and accepted reluctantly by Unionists.

THE ANGLO-IRISH WAR, 1921–2

Sinn Féin's military wing, the Irish Volunteers, reformed itself as the Irish Republican Army (IRA) determined to wage guerrilla war against the British forces. Its numbers have been estimated at about 3000 activists with around 12,000 supporters. Arrayed against them were 40,000 British troops and the Royal Irish Constabulary, reinforced by about 7000 additional English recruits, authorised by Lloyd George. These were divided into the Auxiliaries, recruited from ex-British army officers, and the 'Black and Tans', mainly recruited from non-commissioned soldiers.

The war that ensued was marked by appalling atrocities and acts of deliberate cruelty by both sides, but particularly by the Black and Tans. Their treatment of the Irish, the terror they engendered, and especially their torching of whole villages, drove thousands of Irish into the arms of Sinn Féin and the IRA. The Black and Tans became the hated symbols of British authority in Ireland. Ranged against them were the IRA, protected by the communities within which they operated, and waging war by raids and ambushes. Disguised as civilians, they were difficult to detect and this very fact led to appalling reprisals by the British authorities on whole towns and communities, with many innocent people left dead.

As news of the continuing atrocities filtered through to the British public, demands for a truce grew. The ferocity of the 'Troubles' finally convinced Lloyd George that a constitutional settlement, acceptable to Republicans and Unionists, had to be found. On 11 July 1921, a truce was called and negotiations began.

THE ANGLO-IRISH TREATY 1921

David Lloyd George put together a team of negotiators and invited Irish leaders to London to discuss a settlement. There were four main issues at stake. They were:

- the status of whatever new Irish state emerged
- partition of Ireland
- the use of Irish ports by Britain for the purpose of defence
- the oath of allegiance to the Crown.

Lloyd George used all his skills of diplomacy and duplicity, playing on the belief that he was the last best hope for a settlement. He convinced the Irish that, if he failed, he would be forced to resign and would be replaced by Andrew Bonar Law, a hard-liner. He managed to get them to agree to the appointment of a boundary commission, charged with working out which counties should comprise Ulster, and which Ireland. This was, in fact, a major triumph because it meant that the Republicans had dropped their objection to partition.

Eventually, on 6 December 1921, the Anglo-Irish Treaty was signed:

- Southern Ireland became the Irish Free State and was given dominion status. It had its own Parliament but would remain part of the British Empire and would be loyal to the British Crown.
- The six provinces, Antrim, Armagh, Derry, Down, Fermanagh and Tyrone, formed Northern Ireland and remained part of the United Kingdom
- There was a Council of Ireland, intended to pave the way for a united Ireland.

The existing Parliament of Northern Ireland was given a month in which to decide whether to stay with Britain or go with the Irish Free State. It immediately voted to stay with Britain.

So was this success or failure? Many traditional Conservatives were horrified that control of most of

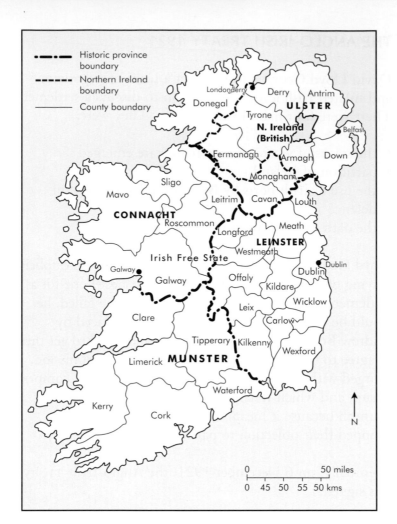

The political division of Ireland after the Government of Ireland Act 1920

Ireland had been given to people they regarded as little better than common gunmen. But they were relieved that Ulster had been safeguarded and that southern Ireland was still tied to the Empire and to the Crown. In the Irish Free State, however, the treaty created deep divisions. Many felt they had been betrayed by their leaders because a true republic had not been proclaimed. The IRA split into Regulars, who supported the treaty, and the Irregulars, whose opposition was only ended in 1923 after a bitter civil war. The solutions provided by the Government of Ireland Act and by the Anglo-Irish Treaty were far from perfect. At best, they provided a breathing space.

SUMMARY QUESTIONS

1 Explain why Gladstone's first two Home Rule bills were unsuccessful.

2 Why was it more likely that the third Home Rule Bill would be successful?

3 What was the significance of the Easter Rising of 1916?

4 Why was partition necessary?

5 Study the cartoon on page 107. How useful would the cartoon be to an historian studying the partition of Ireland?

6 Why do you think that all the proposed 'solutions' to the Irish question between the years 1885 and 1922 were accompanied by violence?

CHAPTER 10

The fall of Lloyd George, 1918–22

The so-called 'coupon election' of December 1918 (see pages 73–6) put David Lloyd George in a peculiar position. He was swept back to power as the leader of the coalition with a large majority (effectively 322) in the Commons over all the other parties combined. Asquith had lost his seat as had three leading Labour Party politicians, Arthur Henderson, James Ramsay MacDonald and Philip Snowden. But Lloyd George was a prime minister without a party. His split with Asquith in 1916 had divided the Liberal Party (see pages 70–1) and his determination to carry the coalition into peace-time politics effectively destroyed the Liberal Party as a potential party of government for the foreseeable future. Lloyd George's power base in the Commons rested on the support of the Conservative Party backbenchers and the goodwill of the Conservative leader, Andrew Bonar Law. They would maintain him in power for just as long as he was useful to them. After all, the Conservatives by themselves had a comfortable majority in the Commons. Lloyd George was only necessary to them for as long as he commanded popular support with the voting public. Realising this, Lloyd George found delegation difficult: he had to be a high-profile leader and he had to be seen to be successful. But while he could claim successes as personal triumphs, the flip-side of these tactics was that disasters had to be seen as personal failures. Lloyd George was in an unstable position, following a high-risk strategy, a strategy that, in the end, did not work.

POLITICAL MANOEUVRINGS

The failure of 'fusion'

David Lloyd George attempted to create a realignment in British politics by trying to achieve an amalgamation (fusion) of the left and centre of the Conservative Party with those Liberals who supported him. In this way, he

would create a genuine centre party in British politics. This wasn't such a strange idea. These Conservatives and Liberals had been working together for over five years. Why should they not form a political party and change the face of British politics?

In March 1920, 95 Conservative MPs petitioned for the development of the coalition into a single political party. This was certainly what Lloyd George wanted. Indeed, in February of that year he had urged Liberal ministers that 'Liberal labels lead nowhere; we must be prepared to burn them.' However, he failed to persuade the coalition Liberals that this was the right way to go. Indeed, although there might have been a parliamentary desire for such a political party, there was little support among rank-and-file party members in the constituencies for such a move.

The resignation of Bonar Law

With the failure of 'fusion', Lloyd George was left dependent upon Conservative backbenchers, ably managed by the Conservative leader Andrew Bonar Law, who was both friend and adviser to Lloyd George. But, in May 1921, Bonar Law resigned because of ill-health, although he stayed on as an MP. He was succeeded as Conservative Party leader by Austen Chamberlain, quite a different sort of leader. Aloof and vain, Chamberlain was out of touch with backbenchers and critical of Lloyd George, whom he thought should resign after the next general election. For the immediate future, however, he was content to support Lloyd George as prime minister, believing that this was essential if Labour were to be kept out of office. Other Conservatives were less charitable, and a right-wing group known as the 'die-hards' had always opposed Lloyd George's premiership and distrusted his policy towards Ireland. Indeed, in January 1922, Neville Chamberlain wrote: 'This dirty little Welsh Attorney and his Coalition Liberal sycophants think they can dictate a policy to the whole Unionist Party.' For Lloyd George, Conservative Party support was always going to be an unreliable card to play.

ECONOMIC PROBLEMS AND THE COLLAPSE OF RECONSTRUCTION

The coalition government was elected in 1918 on a wave of optimism. The horrors of war were in the past; Lloyd George had promised a 'land fit for heroes' and the coalition was going to deliver that promise. Or was it?

The beginnings of a land 'fit for heroes'
- Addison's Housing Act 1919 obliged all local authorities to ensure that people were decently housed. Central government guaranteed to subsidise the cost of local government and private building. The scheme ran up against reluctant local authorities and a shortage of bricklayers and builders who preferred to work on more lucrative schemes. Nevertheless, by July 1921 when Christopher Addison, the minister responsible, resigned, 100,000 subsidised houses had been built; and 170,000 were built during the life of the government.
- In 1920, the Unemployment Act was extended to cover an additional 12 million workers with unemployment insurance, covering most of the wage-earning population. However, agricultural workers, domestic servants and civil servants were still excluded.
- The Agriculture Act 1920 supported agriculture in that it kept the system of price guarantees for wheat and oats introduced in 1917, gave greater protection to tenant farmers and protected agricultural wages.

The collapse of reconstruction
In April 1921, Britain was hit by a slump that saw exports fall to 47.9 per cent of the 1920 figures and 2 million people unemployed. How did that happen? The basic problem was the effect of the war on the British economy:

- 9 per cent of all men under 45 had been killed in the war.
- 1.6 million men had been wounded and many of these never re-entered the job market.
- 150,000 people died in the flu epidemic of 1918–19.
- 3.5 million people were receiving some kind of pension or allowance.

- Many overseas markets had been lost to Britain during the war.
- The war had led to over-investment in the staple industries of iron and steel, coal, shipbuilding and textiles and these products were not needed in such quantities in peacetime.
- Britain owed substantial amounts of money to the USA and was, in turn, owed money by Russia and other allies.

How did Lloyd George and the coalition government react?

At the end of 1921, the government called on ministers to reduce their budgets by £175 million out of a total expenditure of £1136 million. They managed to economise to the tune of £75 million.

Lloyd George set up a committee of businessmen, chaired by Sir Edward Geddes, to advise him and to find the remaining £100 million. The Geddes Committee reported in February 1922 and recommended sweeping cuts in public expenditure: £46.5 million from the armed services and £18.2 million from education, for example. The fact that this latter would have meant classes of 60–70 children seems to have been accepted by Lloyd George with equanimity.

Not for nothing were Geddes' recommendations referred to as the 'Geddes axe'. Future governments, faced with alarming economic problems, too readily reached for the same axe. Hardly the most appropriate action when jobs were disappearing fast.

In the event, this time, what suffered most was the government's programme of reconstruction:

- Addison's housing subsidies were withdrawn.
- The Agriculture Act 1920 was repealed and agricultural wages were left to be determined by market forces.
- The provisions of the Unemployment Act were altered by increasing the time during which benefits could be claimed and increasing the amount of the benefits that could be claimed, but – and this was a big but – requiring claimants to prove that they were genuinely

seeking work. This last requirement led to the creation of vast numbers of local committees to make sure only the genuinely deserving got state help, and caused a great deal of resentment.

INDUSTRIAL UNREST: HOW DID THE GOVERNMENT HANDLE IT?

In the ways in which it handled industrial relations, the coalition government showed the same shift from reconstruction to reaction that it showed in its handling of the economy – and this shift was, too, determined by the performance of the economy. At first, Lloyd George showed all his negotiating skills. He:

- brought the September 1919 rail strike to an end;
- averted the threat of a coal strike in February 1919 by appointing the Sankey Commission to investigate pay and conditions in the coal industry;
- set up industrial councils to negotiate wage rates, hours, training and production methods.

But, once the economic situation deteriorated, and Lloyd George was dependent on the Conservative members of the coalition government, confrontation became the keynote of industrial relations:

- Lloyd George refused to accept the recommendations of the Sankey Commission to nationalise the coal mines;
- troops and tanks were employed to end strikes the government regarded as being politically motivated;
- the recommendations of industrial councils were allowed to die.

Industry didn't take this lying down:

- A general strike seemed likely in the Spring of 1921 when a triple alliance of miners, railwaymen and transport workers united in protest against a mine owner's imposition of a 50 per cent cut in miners' pay. Lloyd George intervened personally and managed to isolate the miners' federation, so splitting the alliance. At the last moment, known as Black Friday, the railwaymen

and transport workers backed down. The miners stayed out on strike until July 1921, when they were forced to go back on the mine owners' terms.
- In 1921, almost 86 million working days were lost because of industrial action.

David Lloyd George's hope of creating a national consensus that would unite the classes had failed. He could no longer be seen as a champion of national unity.

CORRUPTION AND SCANDAL?

In the somewhat messy world of politics, where principle is often sacrificed to expediency, David Lloyd George had never enjoyed a reputation for straight dealing and absolute honesty. In his career as a politician, he managed to outrage different groups of his colleagues and different sections of society at large:

- He relied on friends and personal advisers rather than the cabinet and civil service.
- He rarely attended the House of Commons and in September 1921 he summoned a cabinet meeting in Inverness Town Hall so that he didn't have to interrupt his Scottish holiday by making the long journey to London.
- He leaked secret information to the press.
- He had a wife and a mistress (Frances Stevenson, his secretary) and was rumoured to be unfaithful to both. Not for nothing was his nickname 'the goat'.

The Lloyd George fund
But all this was nothing compared to the scandal that broke over the 'Lloyd George fund'. It had been long accepted that large donations to a political party could be rewarded with a peerage after a decent interval of time. Lloyd George took this practice to new depths and openly offered honours for sale. It was said that, in the coalition years, a knighthood could be bought for £10,000–£12,000 and a baronetcy for £35,000–£40,000. During this time, some 90 peerages and 20,000 OBEs were bought by wealthy, if not deserving, individuals. This wasn't done in secret behind closed doors, but openly using agents to

organise the sale of honours and titles on a commission basis. When challenged in a Commons debate, Lloyd George argued that this was a perfectly justifiable way of raising political funds, given that he didn't have wealthy backers like the Conservatives, nor money from the trade unions, like the Labour Party. There was a certain amount of hypocrisy in Conservative outrage over the sale of honours: the party pocketed half the money raised in this way. But, nevertheless, once a prime minister is believed to be dishonest they become almost unelectable.

THE END GAME

Lloyd George himself brought matters to a head by announcing his intention to call a general election. This was the Conservatives' chance to back him, or sack him.

The Carlton Club meeting

The Carlton Club was the meeting place of all prominent Conservative politicians. On 19 October 1922, Austen Chamberlain called a party meeting there with the object of deciding how to go forward into the general election. Here, he demonstrated his lack of leadership by urging support for Lloyd George in the forthcoming election without feeling it necessary to mention his intention of dropping him as premier once the coalition government had been re-elected. Much more impressive was Stanley Baldwin a junior minister in the coalition government:

> *[Lloyd George] is a dynamic force and it is from this very fact that our troubles, in my opinion, arise. A dynamic force is a very terrible thing; it may crush you but it is not necessarily right. It is owing to that dynamic force, and that remarkable personality, that the Liberal Party, to which he formally belonged, has been smashed to pieces; and it is my firm conviction that, in time, the same thing will happen to our party. I would like to give you just one illustration to show what I mean by the disintegrating influence of a dynamic force. Take Mr Chamberlain and myself. We stand here today, he prepared to go into the wilderness if he should be compelled to forsake the Prime Minister, and I prepared to go into the wilderness if I should be compelled to go with him.*

Results of the 1922 general election

	Seats won	Total votes	% vote
Conservatives	345	5,500,382	38.2
Labour	142	4,241,383	29.5
Lloyd George Liberals	62	1,673,240	11.6
Asquithian Liberals	54	2,516,287	17.5

The Conservative MPs voted by 187 to 87 to abandon Lloyd George and fight the forthcoming general election as the Conservative Party, unencumbered by any thoughts of coalition.

Results of the 1922 general election

The election results, devastating for the Liberals, speak for themselves. The Liberals, whether Asquithians or supporters of Lloyd George, were reassured. Labour emerged as an electable party and a future contender for government. David Lloyd George resigned and, after nearly seventeen years of service in the cabinet, never again held office.

This cartoon was published in *Punch* magazine in 1920

THE SCAPEGOAT THAT TURNED.

["If I am driven alone into the Wilderness . . . . " - *Mr. Lloyd George at Manchester.*
"My husband thoroughly enjoys a fight." - *Mrs. Lloyd George at East Ham.*]

SUMMARY QUESTIONS

1 How far can Lloyd George's attempt at 'fusion' be seen as an attempt to build himself a power base?

2 What were the successes of the coalition government 1918–22?

3 Would you agree with the view that the coalition government of 1918–22 failed because of the economic slump?

4 Study the cartoon 'The Scapegoat that Turned'. What is the message of the cartoon?

5 How far was David Lloyd George the architect of his own downfall?

CHAPTER 11

The General Strike of 1926: revolution or muddle?

At midnight on 3 May 1926, about 3 million people throughout Britain stopped work indefinitely in the first nationwide strike ever to occur in Britain. It damaged relationships between government and trade unions for years to come, caused inter-union mistrust and left a legacy of bitterness and the sour taste of class warfare. Was the government, as it wished people to believe, facing revolution? Or had it simply muddled its way into the General Strike?

PROBLEMS IN THE COAL INDUSTRY

Working in the mines
The General Strike started with problems in the coal industry. More than any other industry, conditions there were poor and pay was low. Yet it was the only British industry employing more than 1 million workers. The miners' union, the Miners Federation of Great Britain (MFGB) was well-organised with a tradition of militancy and a large number of self-educated members who had socialist tendencies. Mining towns and villages tended to be close-knit social communities, born of male interdependence in the pits. This enabled them to act in defence of their own interests, presenting a genuinely united front, to the admiration of other industries and to a certain amount of exasperation with what could be seen as stubbornness and blind stupidity.

Noah Ablett, an executive member of the MFGB, described in 1922 what it was like to be a miner:

> *The hewer down the mine, away from the sunlight and fresh air, sometimes up to a temperature of 90 degrees, every moment of the day inhaling coal and shale dust, perspiring so abnormally as few men in other industries can realise; head*

throbbing with the almost inhuman exertion; the roof, perhaps eighteen inches low, perhaps twenty feet high; ears constantly strained for movements in the strata on which his limbs or his life is dependent, liable always to wounds and death from falls of roof and sides, and ever and over all the sickening dread of the awful explosion; such a man is entitled to our sympathy and our respect, but what he frequently gets is abuse.

Between 1922 and 1924, 3603 miners were killed and 597,158 injured. This was, indeed, a dangerous industry on which all others depended for their source of power.

Troubled times

In 1925, the coal industry was in trouble. Indeed, the only postwar years of prosperity for the industry were the result of a crisis in Europe. In the years 1923–4, French troops occupied the Ruhr coalfield because Germany had defaulted on its reparations payments, and German exports of coal stopped. British exports filled the gap left in the international market for coal. However, the **Dawes Plan** settled the reparations dispute between France and Germany, and German exports of coal began again.

The position of the British coal industry was further exacerbated when Winston Churchill, Chancellor of the Exchequer in Stanley Baldwin's Conservative government, put Britain back on to the **gold standard in 1925**. This had the effect of raising the prices of all British exports by about 10 per cent. The effect of these two events on the coal industry was catastrophic. In the first six months of 1925, it made a loss of £2.1 million.

What did the mine owners do?

The mine owners acted decisively by attempting to cut costs. They:

- gave the miners one month's notice that their 1924 wages agreement would end
- lengthened the miners' working day to eight hours
- reduced miners' pay by 13–38 per cent.

In order fully to understand the impact this had on the

The Dawes Plan 1924 Part of the settlement after the First World War involved Germany making payments, called reparations, to the Allies. When Germany defaulted on payments to France, French troops occupied the German Ruhr coalfield between January 1923 and August 1924. The Dawes Committee, named after its American chairman, came up with the Dawes Plan, restructuring the reparation payments and making Germany a £40 million loan. Reparation payments began again and the French troops withdrew.

The gold standard A system whereby each country fixed its currency value to a particular amount of gold, so that there would be fixed exchange rates. This system traditionally provided industrial stability because profits depended on the amount sold, and would not vary as interest rates varied.

mining industry, we have to go back to the relatively prosperous days of 1923–4.

Pay In May 1924, the mine owners and the Miners Federation of Great Britain, prompted by the Labour government, negotiated a national wages agreement. This resulted in the first improvements for miners since the end of the 1914–18 war. However, although claims were made on a national basis by the MFGB, miners were paid different wages according to the coalfield, or district, in which they worked and this resulted in huge regional differences. There had been attempts to change this. In 1921, a National Board was set up and the miners had hoped it would set a standard wage throughout the industry, but the owners were implacably against this. Evan Williams, on behalf of the owners, explained, in response to the request that the 1921 pay claim be applied equally to all miners:

> *It would be bad for the trade as a whole. The general efficiency of the industry would decline because the incentive to remain efficient would disappear once it were established that the skill and energy of the good concerns were to be used to subsidise the inefficiency and indifference of the poor concerns.*

In the end, the National Board was able to fix guidelines only for the district boards. Against this background, to have to accept a cut in wages of as much as 38 per cent in some districts, was unacceptable to the miners but regarded by the owners as the only possible reaction to the huge fall in profits.

Hours The miners were in a similar situation with regard to working hours. An Act of 1908 limited the number of hours they could work underground to eight. In 1919, this had been further reduced to seven hours a day, with the intention of lowering it to six hours as soon as the industry was in a sound economic position. This hadn't happened, but inevitably an increase in hours to eight was seen by the miners as a retrograde measure, but by the owners as the only possible way forward.

	Average earnings per man-shift		% earnings over 1914
	Shillings	pence	
1914	6	6	0%
May 1925 earnings	10	8	64.5%
Owners' offer	8	11	37.84%
(to be paid from August 1925)			

Changes in average earnings of miners

How did the miners react?

Not surprisingly, the miners reacted angrily. The proposed terms of the new agreement were sent to the Miners Federation of Great Britain on 1 July. The MFGB rejected the owners' proposal immediately. Its secretary A.J. Cook declared: 'Not a penny off the pay, not a minute on the day.' In a deliberate attempt to develop an industrial alliance in order to strengthen its hand, the MFGB turned to the Trades Union Congress (TUC) for help.

What was the TUC's response?

The General Council of the TUC backed the miners' case. This was partly because it had genuine sympathy for them but also because the TUC was afraid that an attack on miners' wages would presage a general attack on wages across a range of occupations. The TUC gave this statement to the press on 11 July 1925:

> The terms put forward [by the mine owners] propose drastic reductions in the already meagre wages paid to the miners, abolish the principle of a minimum wage, destroy the principle of national agreements, make the national unification of the industry an impossibility, and would, if carried to their logical conclusion, eventually lead to settlements between individual companies and their workers and cause chaos within the industry.
>
> The General Council [of the TUC] appreciate to the full the fact that no self-respecting body of organised workers could negotiate on such terms.

The General Council particularly approve of the steadfast opposition of the Miners Federation to any proposals for a lengthening of the working day.

The General Council are confident they will have the backing of the whole organised Trade Union Movement in placing themselves unreservedly at the disposal of the Miners Federation to assist the Federation in any way possible.

A Trade Union Congress on Unemployment had coincidently been arranged in London for 24 July. The miners' leaders once again put their case and once again received the full support of the trade union movement. The TUC set up a special committee to organise support for the miners, and agreed to ban all movements of coal:

Official Instructions to All Railway and Transport Workers

Railways: Wagons containing coal must not be attached to any train after midnight on Friday July 31st.

Docks, Wharves etc: A general stoppage of men handling coal on other classes of tonnage on Friday midnight.

Road transport: All men engaged in delivering coal to commercial and industrial concerns will cease Friday night July 31st.

Signed by the Presidents and Secretaries of ASLEF, NUR, RCA, T&GWU, TUC General Council.

Red Friday

The government, meanwhile, was working behind the scenes to try to avert trouble. Meetings were held with the TUC and with the mine owners, represented by the Mining Association. It quickly became clear that the miners would not budge, despite Prime Minister Stanley Baldwin's assurances that the government would not grant any subsidy to the mining industry, which had to 'stand on its own foundations'. Finally, in the early hours of Friday 31 July, the government decided to play for time and changed its collective mind. The mining industry was offered a subsidy for nine months (totalling £23 million) so that the miners would not have to accept pay cuts

immediately and the government offered to set up a
committee of enquiry, to report in the spring of 1926.

The TUC was jubilant. No embargo was placed on the
movement of coal: the threat to do so was enough to make
the government back down. The day on which the TUC
forced a government to change its mind became known as
'Red Friday'.

Reactions to Red Friday were, however, indicative of
trouble ahead. The miners' reaction is illustrated by the
words of the chairman of the MFGB delegate conference
on 19 August 1925:

> We have no need to glorify about a victory. It is only an
> armistice, and it will depend largely how we stand between
> now and May 1st next year [when the subsidy was due to
> end] as an organisation in respect to unity as to what will be
> the ultimate result.

The TUC took a broader and almost naively optimistic
view:

> The manifestation of solidarity which has been exhibited by
> all sections of the Trade Union Movement is a striking
> portent for the future and marks an epoch in the history of
> the Movement.

> While there is little doubt that the conflict has been avoided,
> the Trade Union Movement must be alert and vigilant in
> case the necessity should again arise for it to act in defence of
> its standards.

The mine owners, on the other hand, condemned and
prepared for action:

> Mr Baldwin has secured the support of the House of
> Commons for his policy of Danegeld. No inquiry can put into
> the industry money which is not there, compel our foreign
> customers to buy coal they can obtain more cheaply elsewhere
> or enable the industry to pay wages out of nothing. We warn
> the public that the crisis will occur in exactly the same form
> next May unless the situation is resolutely faced in the

interim. It will be the endeavour of the mining association to expose the activities of our English Reds, the methods by which they control the Miners Federation and other unions, and their policy towards industry and the state.

The Samuel Commission

Members of the Samuel Commission were appointed in September 1925 and were due to report six months later. There were four members:

- Sir Herbert Samuel, who had served in the Liberal government from 1906 and who had previously been British High Commissioner in Palestine
- Sir William Beveridge, a former civil servant and director of the London School of Economics
- General the Honourable Sir Herbert Lawrence, managing partner of the bankers Glyn Mills & Co.
- Mr Kenneth Lee, chairman of Tootal, Broadhurst & Lee, cotton manufacturers, and chairman of the District Bank.

The Samuel Commission reported in March 1926. It made several general recommendations that were favourable to the miners:

- amalgamation of some pits in order to provide better facilities (pit-head baths, for example) and to eliminate inefficient pits
- the seven-hour working day to remain
- better industrial relations through the introduction of pit-head committees
- profit sharing
- holidays with pay.

But this was in the future. What the miners had to accept, immediately, was a reduction in pay but no increase in their working hours.

In the meantime, the government had been working hard behind the scenes, preparing for what some members believed was an inevitable, head-on clash with the TUC. The country was divided into ten areas, each under the control of a civil commissioner. Local authorities were informed in November 1925 about what was happening, and conferences were held in December and January to coordinate the work of national and local officials. The government was preparing for a general strike.

Countdown to disaster

The government had agreed to implement the findings of the Samuel Commission provided both mine owners and miners accepted it, too. This proved impossible.

- The MFGB met with the owners' Miners Association on 20 and 26 March and 1 April without being able to reach any agreement. The owners' final offer was an eight-hour day and a minimum wage that was 20 per cent above the 1914 level. This was unacceptable to the miners.
- The TUC tried to persuade the miners to accept the Samuel Commission's recommendations about reorganisation of the industry in exchange for temporary wage reductions, but to no avail.
- On Friday 3 April the miners, having refused the owners' final offer, were locked out.
- MFGB union executives voted, on behalf of their members, by 3,653,527 to 49,911 in favour of 'coordinated action' to begin at midnight on 3 May.
- The government and the TUC sought desperately for a solution or at least a stay of execution. A negotiating committee, consisting of three members of the government and three members of the TUC General Council, met at 8 o'clock on the evening of Saturday 1 May. After five hours of talks, they came up with a form of words they hoped would satisfy both the MFGB and the Miners Association. Negotiations were to continue on the basis of the Samuel Commission's report provided the owners ended the lock-out.
- On Sunday morning, 2 May, the TUC General Council met to consider the proposed 'solution'. The MFGB representatives were angry that they hadn't been consulted beforehand and refused to accept the compromise.
- At the same time, the cabinet met to discuss the proposed 'solution' and were dismayed to learn from the postmaster-general that strike notices had already been sent out.

Daily Mail The key passage in the *Daily Mail* that the printers refused to print was:

The miners, after weeks of negotiation, have declined the proposals made to them and the coalfields of Britain are idle.

The Council of the Trades Union Congress, which represents all the other trade unions, has determined to support the miners by going to the extreme of calling a General Strike.

We do not wish to say anything hard about the miners themselves. As to their leaders, all we need say at this moment is that some of them are (and have openly declared themselves) under the influence of people who mean no good to this country.

The General Strike is not an industrial dispute; it is a revolutionary movement, intended to inflict suffering on the great mass of innocent persons in the community and thereby put forcible constraint upon the government.

- A final, desperate meeting was held between the two groups at 11.00pm on Sunday. They were working towards a new form of words that they hoped would be acceptable to both sides when word came that the Daily Mail printers were refusing to print an editorial condemning the strike. That was it. Stanley Baldwin announced that negotiations were at an end because of 'overt acts' that had taken place, including 'gross interference with the freedom of the press'. The TUC representatives were astounded. The printers' refusal had been unauthorised and this was the first they had heard of it. But, by the time they had written a repudiation of the printers' actions, Baldwin had gone to bed and the other cabinet members had gone home.

The General Strike was about to begin.

A CHALLENGE TO THE CONSTITUTION OR AN INDUSTRIAL DISPUTE?

On 3 May 1926, the TUC called the workers out on strike, industry by industry: dockers, iron and steel workers, workers in heavy chemicals, railwaymen, workers in the building trades and in electricity and gas industries. The TUC had no plans beyond a simple stoppage of work and so the many local strike committees that sprung up had little to do but ensure that the strike was solid and no damage was done to life or property. The TUC's offer to maintain the distribution of food supplies was ignored by the government.

Unlike the TUC, the government had carefully prepared plans for such an emergency, and they swung into action immediately. King George V declared a state of emergency and the government invoked the Emergency Powers Act. It swore in over 200,000 special constables (who were hardly needed) and set the army to keep the power stations going, escort food convoys and generally help the police. Using the Organisation for the Maintenance of Supplies, the government recruited volunteers to drive buses and trains and to unload ships. Many university undergraduates and young men who would never in their wildest dreams think

Part of the government precautions against civil unrest: a tank in Hyde Park on 10 May 1926

of doing such work, had 'jolly fun' driving convoys of lorries from the docks or keeping a skeleton bus service running.

Stanley Baldwin's government was determined to present the strike as an attack on constitutional government – an attempt at revolution. The government produced a newspaper *The British Gazette* which put across its point of view in a somewhat alarmist way; it also had access to the BBC. On 6 May Baldwin wrote in the *British Gazette*:

> *Constitutional government is being attacked.*
>
> *Let all good citizens whose livelihood and labour have thus been put in peril bear with fortitude and patience the hardships with which they have been so suddenly confronted.*
>
> *Stand behind the government, who are doing their part, confident that you will co-operate in the measures they have undertaken to preserve the liberties and privileges of the people of these islands.*
>
> *The laws of England are the people's birthright.*
>
> *The laws are in your keeping.*
>
> *You have made Parliament their guardian.*
>
> *The general strike is a challenge to Parliament and is the road to anarchy and ruin.*

The trade unions, with far less money and fewer resources, published the *British Worker* in order to present their case to the country.

> *The workers must not be misled by Mr Baldwin's renewed attempt last night to represent the present strike as a political issue. The trade unions are fighting for one thing, and one thing only – to protect the miners' standard of life. The Prime Minister pleads for peace but insists that the General Council is challenging the Constitution. That is untrue.*
>
> *The General Council does not challenge one rule, law or custom of the Constitution; it asks only that the miners be safeguarded.*

Between 4 and 12 May, a propaganda battle was played out between the TUC and the government. Both sides adopted over-simplified positions in public. The TUC was clearly not overtly challenging the constitution, but then neither was it simply acting only in the interests of the miners. It was trying to force a legally and constitutionally elected government to change its mind. The TUC was a force in the land and it was using its considerable power. Magazines, newspapers, magistrates, vicars and even the Archbishop of Canterbury had their say.

Not with a bang but a whimper

Behind the scenes, the TUC and the government were working almost continuously to find a solution. Moderate trade unionists were horrified to find themselves leading their movement into conflict with a lawfully elected government. Moderate members of the government were equally horrified to find that a substantial number of people believed the country was close to revolution:

- Sir Herbert Samuel returned from Italy and offered to act as mediator between the parties. The government would not authorise him to speak on its behalf, but the TUC was desperate to talk to him. The deadlock had to be broken and the TUC didn't think it could win.
- On 10 May, Samuel produced the Samuel Memorandum. It proposed:
  - negotiations should resume
  - the subsidy should be renewed

THE LEVER BREAKS.

This cartoon 'The Lever Breaks' was published in *Punch* magazine in May 1926

- disputes should be referred to a National Wages Board
- no revision of wages until the Board was convinced that the Samuel report's recommendations regarding reorganisation would be adopted.
- The General Council, mightily relieved, was willing to accept the Samuel Memorandum as the basis for calling off the strike.
- The miners were not: they were furious.
- The government didn't commit itself either way.
- On the evening of 11 May, Baldwin invited members of the TUC General Council to meet him in Downing Street. With nothing new to offer, he assured them that he would try for a just and lasting settlement.

Reassured, and relieved to have found an excuse, on 12 May the TUC called off the General Strike. There was genuine horror and disbelief among the strikers. They thought they were winning: winning not just for themselves but for the miners. In some areas the strikers heard the news that the General Strike was over and assumed they had won and the government had climbed down. The miners, embittered and disillusioned, were left to fight on alone.

What happened to the miners?

The TUC could not persuade the miners to return to work. Baldwin's offers to negotiate came to nothing. The lock-out notices were not withdrawn. On 1 July, Parliament passed an act suspending the seven-hour day and allowing the mine owners to impose an eight-hour shift if they wished. The lock-out continued officially until November, but the more prosperous coalfields saw a trickle of miners returning in August. Gradually, most miners returned to the pits, driven there by hunger and poverty. District agreements on wages were reintroduced and, although these varied from coalfield to coalfield, most imposed the eight-hour day and the reduction in pay averaged 13 per cent. Every miner returned to work on longer hours and lower wages.

What happened to the returning strikers in other industries?

The General Council of the TUC had failed to negotiate terms on which the strikers could return to work. The government issued a statement:

> *His Majesty's Government have no power to compel employers to take back every man who has been on strike, nor have they entered into any obligation of any kind on this matter.*

Many employers interpreted this as meaning they were free to re-employ strikers on lower wages – and they did just that. In many cases, strikers were only re-employed if they guaranteed not to join a union. Other employers singled out the ringleaders and refused to engage them again. The railway companies took a particularly hard stand; London County Council gave the men different, lower paid jobs; the Admiralty took between two to four years' pension entitlement away from returning strikers. And so it went on. Arthur Henderson recited a long list in the House of Commons. That this should be happening within 48 hours of a return to work horrified both the TUC and the Prime Minister. Baldwin issued a statement:

> *I will not countenance any attack on the part of any employers to use this present occasion for trying in any way to get reductions in wages below those in force before the strike, or any increase in hours.*

How did the TUC General Council react?

Baldwin's difficulties were nothing compared to those of the TUC General Council. The telegrams it sent out calling off the strike instructed each union to make its own arrangements for a return to work. When the local strike committees discovered what had really happened, their anger erupted. There was violence on the picket lines and TUC leaders were accused of timidity, treachery and worse. The trade union movement was disintegrating around them. Twenty-four hours after the strike officially ended, the number of strikers had increased by 100,000. The TUC General Council tried to retrieve the situation by issuing a statement saying that it had responded to the government's call for peace and that the trade union movement was not broken. Telegrams were sent to individual unions stating that the 'General Strike has ended. It has not failed.' A debatable point.

Did the strikers go back on the employers' terms?

The strikers remembered what the TUC General Council had forgotten: that in unity lay strength. In Manchester, 30,000 railway workers demonstrated, demanding unconditional reinstatement; in Hull, railway workers, tramway workers and dockers refused to go back to work because 150 employees were threatened with dismissal. The BBC reported that there was no general return to work as those involved in the General Strike held out for unconditional reinstatement. But these protests were short-lived. Unions had to make their own peace with their employers and many workers returned on worse terms and conditions than they had had before the strike.

WHAT WERE THE EFFECTS OF THE GENERAL STRIKE?

The effects of the General Strike were immediate and damaging. Quantifiable results are relatively easy to calculate:

- 162 million working days were lost.
- Coal exports fell from 54.5 million tons in 1925 to 20.5 million tons in 1926.

- Trade union membership fell from 8.3 million in 1920, to 5.3 million in 1926, to 4.3 million in 1933.
- Total losses, including wages, have been put at over £200 million.
- The Trades Dispute Act 1927 prevented workers in industries not directly affected by a dispute from coming out on strike in sympathy. This effectively ended any possibility of another General Strike. The Act also changed the rules about the way in which unions paid money to the Labour Party. Only part of any one union subscription could be passed on, and then only with the written consent of the union member concerned. This change from contracting-out to contracting-in hit hard at Labour Party funds.

However, the most lasting effect was that of bitterness and distrust between employer and employee, between union member and the TUC and between workers and the government.

SUMMARY QUESTIONS

1 Why did problems in the mining industry lead to the General Strike?

2 Look at the Punch cartoon on page 132. What point is the artist making?
  Is he on the side of the government or the strikers?

3 Who was to blame for the General Strike?

4 How useful were the contributions to the situation made by Sir Herbert Samuel?

5 Did Stanley Baldwin handle the situation well?

6 How close to revolution was Britain in 1926?

7 Did the striking workers ever really stand a chance of winning?

8 What, in your estimation, was the most important outcome of the General Strike?

CHAPTER 12

The rise of the Labour Party, 1900–24

In the general election of 1900, the Labour Party (then called the Labour Representative Committee) polled only 1.8 per cent of the total vote. Twenty-four years later, James Ramsay MacDonald became Prime Minister in the first Labour government. What had happened in those 24 years to bring about such a change in the party's fortunes? You will have read various references to the Labour Party in the years to 1924, and it is now time to draw all those threads together and consider the cataclysmic shift in British politics that the creation of a new, and ultimately successful, political party wrought.

BEGINNINGS: FROM LABOUR REPRESENTATION COMMITTEE TO LABOUR PARTY, 1900–6

The parliamentary reform acts of 1867 and 1884 gave the vote to an increasing number of working-class men, and it had been the hope and expectation of leading Liberals that they would gravitate naturally to the Liberal Party. However, it wasn't quite that simple.

Did the local Liberal associations welcome working-class men?

Far too many local associations failed to realise the long-term importance of attracting working-class support. The associations tended to be run by local businessmen who did not always welcome working men as likely candidates for election. For example:

- In 1888, the local Mid-Lanark Liberal association turned down a local working-man, Keir Hardie, in favour of an outsider – a Welsh lawyer.
- In 1894, the Southampton Liberals turned down James Ramsay MacDonald, a working-class man who had been working as a private secretary to a leading London Liberal MP.

KEY PERSON

James Ramsay MacDonald (1866–1937) Born the illegitimate son of a Scottish servant girl, as a young man he worked as a clerk in London, and became private secretary to Thomas Lough, a Liberal MP. This brought him into touch with prominent, radical socialist thinkers such as the Fabians, and in 1894 he joined the Independent Labour Party. Believing that Labour should seek power through its own efforts and not by alliance with the Liberal Party, he played a leading part in the formation of the Labour Representation Committee. Working as its secretary (1900–5) and then as the secretary of the Labour Party, he became an MP in 1906 and leader of the parliamentary party in 1911. He resigned as leader in 1914 because of his pacifism, and lost his seat in the 1918 'coupon election'. He returned in 1922 and again led the parliamentary party, becoming Britain's first Labour Prime Minister in 1924. He was Prime Minister again in Labour's second minority government of 1929–31. However, by refusing to resign with his colleagues, and instead leading a National Government with Conservative and Liberal support and then campaigning against the Labour Party, he put himself into the political wilderness for ever. Branded a traitor, he was expelled from the party he had done so much to build up. He remained Prime Minister until 1935 when he became President of the Council until his death in 1937.

The Social Democratic Federation Established in June 1881 by H.M. Hyndman, it claimed to be genuinely Marxist in its aims although it was never supported by Marx or Engels. A small group, it was active mainly in London where it gave many young trade unionists an introduction to socialism. Hyndman and the SDF helped create the LRC, although they pulled out a year later, denouncing Labour as being insufficiently dedicated to the class war. Hyndman apparently alienated working people by his extremism and his habit of quoting from Virgil in Latin in his speeches.

The lessons are obvious. By rejecting able and independently minded working-class men as prospective candidates, the Liberal Party inadvertently created a climate in which Labour, as a distinct and separate political party, could get established. In fact, Keir Hardie went on to be a major force in founding the Labour Party and **Ramsay MacDonald** became, in 1924, the first Labour Prime Minister.

The Labour Representation Committee

By 1900, various left-wing socialist organisations were in operation, the main ones being the **Social Democratic Federation**, the Fabians (see page 40) and the Independent Labour Party (see page 41). Coincidentally, the Trades Union Congress was becoming increasingly worried by the aggressive, anti-union activities of many employers. At its annual conference in 1899, the TUC agreed to call a separate conference to plan for labour representation in Parliament. There was nothing intrinsically revolutionary in this. Most TUC leaders were deeply suspicious of socialism and its radical comrade, Marxism, and were interested simply in obtaining better working conditions for their members. Radical socialists, looking for the reordering of society, were a tiny minority of those interested in parliamentary representation for the working class.

In February 1900, 129 delegates attended the TUC conference held in the Farringdon Memorial Hall, London, and agreed to form a 'distinct Labour group in Parliament'. They set up the Labour Representation Committee to work out how this could be done.

The 1900 election

Almost immediately, the LRC had to fight a general election. It was extremely weak, with no clear political programme and very little money. The only union support came from the Amalgamated Society of Railway Servants, a couple of printers' unions and the Boot and Shoe Workers. Two LRC MPs were elected: Keir Hardie and Richard Bell. But they failed to make much impression. Eight Lib–Lab MPs claimed to be able to speak for working-class people just as authentically as the LRC members.

Taff Vale as a turning point

The Taff Vale decision of 1901 (see page 17) severely undermined the right to strike, as unions were deemed liable to pay unlimited damages to their employers for any revenue lost because of a strike. The financial resources of all unions were under threat and their ability to fight for the rights of their members severely curtailed. But this worked to the advantage of the LRC. The unions realised that they needed representation in Parliament and swung behind the Labour Representation Committee. Between 1901 and 1903, all the major unions, with the exception of the miners, gave the LRC their support. Union membership of the LRC increased from 376,000 in 1901 to 861,000 in 1903 and its funding increased proportionately.

Support from the Liberals

Prior to the 1906 election, the Liberal chief whip, Herbert Gladstone, determined to keep the Conservatives from power, had a secret agreement with Ramsay MacDonald. They agreed not to split the anti-Conservative vote. In practice this meant that in constituencies where a Conservative MP had grown deeply unpopular and was likely to lose his seat in the forthcoming election, he would be opposed by either a Liberal or an LRC candidate, but not both. In the Liberal landslide of 1906 (see page 17) the LRC did very well indeed. It ended up with 29 MPs, including Keir Hardie and Ramsay MacDonald. Seven were **sponsored** by the ILP and the other 22 by trade unions or other local organisations. Once at Westminster, they renamed themselves the Labour Party.

WHAT WAS THE IMPACT OF THE LABOUR PARTY IN PARLIAMENT, 1906–14?

Did the Labour Party influence the Liberal reforms, 1906–12?

In November 1904, David Lloyd George made this speech to the Liberal Party faithful in Manchester:

We have a great Labour party sprung up. Unless we can prove, as I think we can, that there is no necessity for a separate party in order to press forward the legitimate claims of labour, then you will find that the Liberal Party will be

*practically wiped out. In its place, you will get a more
extreme and revolutionary party, which will sail under the
colours of Socialism or Independent Labour.*

*I think it better that you should have a Party which combines
every section and shade of progressive opinion, taken from all
classes of the community, rather than a party which represents
one shade of opinion alone and one class of the community. It
rests with the Liberal Administration to prevent such a state
of things from coming about.*

Did the Liberals, pushed, prodded and cajoled by David
Lloyd George and Winston Churchill, embark upon their
programme of social reform out of fear of the rise of
Labour as a political force? Maybe. But, in the event, the
huge Liberal majority had the effect of drowning out the
voice of Labour. The only 'reform' the Labour Party
persuaded the Liberals to pass was the 1906 Trades
Disputes Act, which restored the pre-Taff Vale position to
the unions. Unions could now picket peacefully and
employers could not sue them for damages. The raft of
Liberal reforms, although not exactly what the Labour
Party would have introduced, could hardly be opposed by
a party committed to improving the lot of working people.

The Labour Party won 29 seats in the 1906 Parliament. By
1914, there were 42 Labour MPs at Westminster. But the
increase in Labour seats was more apparent than real.
Sixteen MPs, sponsored by the miners, had switched from
the Lib–Labs in 1909. Consequentially, the January 1910
election meant an actual loss of five seats. There is
evidence, therefore, that electoral support for Labour was
either static or declining. By 1914, Labour Party MPs
probably had less influence in Parliament than they had
had in 1906.

Why was the early Labour Party so weak?
The Labour Party was perceived as being weak just because
the Liberal Party was so strong. But there were other
reasons:

• The new Labour MPs were working men with limited
  formal education. They found the experience of the

House of Commons, with its formal debating and committees, intimidating.

- The Labour Party was far from a cohesive unit. It was a combination of ILP socialists and trade union officials who had as much sympathy with the Lib–Labs as they had with the socialists.
- A strong leader capable of holding Labour MPs together was needed, but the Labour Party rule of electing a chairman on an annual basis was unlikely to deliver this. The chairman the parliamentary party did elect (1906–8) was Keir Hardie – a charismatic man and great at rallying support, but lacking the patience to mould a team together into a sound parliamentary party.
- Keir Hardie relied a great deal on the solid, sensible and dependable **Arthur Henderson** who was his chief whip. In 1911, Ramsay MacDonald took over as chairman and Arthur Henderson became the Labour Party secretary. Henderson was a man with excellent administrative abilities which, combined with patience and tact, enabled him to forge a cohesive party that was able to contain even the rather troublesome but extremely able Philip Snowden and George Lansbury. However, Henderson's main weakness, in the eyes of some of his colleagues, was his closeness to the Liberals.
- The Osborne judgement of 1909 (see page 62) came as an unexpected blow. MPs were not paid a salary by the state and so were supported by their unions. It took four years for the Liberal government to put matters straight. In 1911, it approved the payment of MPs (£400 per year) and, in 1913, the Trade Union Act permitted trade unions to levy money from their members for political purposes.
- The Osborne judgement meant that the Labour Party had to fight the two elections of 1910 (see pages 33–34) in the midst of a financial crisis, which made it even more dependent on the Liberal Party.

How popular was Labour in the country outside Parliament?

At the local level, the Labour movement was thriving:

- From 1906 to 1914, trade union membership increased from 900,000 to 1,500,000.

Poster urging electors in South Wales to vote for Keir Hardie

A grandiose example of electoral propaganda. Hardie's Election address 1910.

- From 1906 to 1914, membership of socialist societies rose from 17,000 to 33,000.
- In 1906, there were 83 local Labour organisations; by 1914 there were 158.
- By 1914, Labour had a national agent, with seven staff, to coordinate party activities.

The Labour Party was well-prepared to fight the 1915 election. It planned to field at least 100 candidates and intended to win every one of those 100 seats.

HOW DID THE FIRST WORLD WAR (1914–18) AFFECT THE LABOUR PARTY?

The First World War strengthened both the Labour Party and the trade unions. This was largely because the parties of government recognised the need to involve the representatives of working people in the decision-making process and in the war on the Home Front.

Labour MPs in government

When war broke out in 1914, the Labour Party had 42 members in the House of Commons. This could hardly lead them to believe they had a right to be involved in the government of the war, but Asquith thought otherwise. A cooperative working class was essential to the war effort, and in many ways the Labour Party was the political wing of the trade unions.

Ramsay MacDonald having resigned as the leader of the Labour Party because of his pacifist views, Arthur Henderson joined Asquith's first coalition government as President of the Board of Education. When Lloyd George succeeded Asquith as Prime Minister (see page 70) he put Henderson in the war cabinet and appointed eight Labour MPs to other posts, of whom the most important were G.N. Barnes to the Ministry of Pensions, J. Hodge to the Ministry of Labour and J.R. Clynes in succession to Lord Rhondda as food controller. This gave a significant number of Labour MPs direct experience of government.

Trade unions

The cooperation of the trade unions was essential if war production was to proceed unhampered. Government ministers spent many hours persuading trade union officials to agree to dilution, the avoidance of strikes and restrictive practices, and conscription. While this is discussed in greater detail on pages 80–2, it is important to note here that this obviously increased the bargaining power of trade union officials, gave them experience in the practicalities of hard-headed bargaining, and elevated the TUC to a position of authority it had never previously attained.

Did the Labour Party split over the war?

War inevitably creates political tensions, and here the Labour Party was more vulnerable than most. How could a party dedicated to improving the lot of working people possibly connive in the sending of the working people of one nation to fight the working people of another?

Continental left-wing socialist parties were torn apart over this issue. The British Labour Party emerged from the war unscathed and united. How?

- Ramsay MacDonald was a key figure, and his resignation could easily have split the Labour Party. At the very least, because of his pacifism, opprobrium that was piled on the heads of pacifists by the general public could have attached itself to the Labour Paty as well. MacDonald did suffer from vitriolic abuse, much of it from trade unionists, but the dignified way in which he upheld his principles did, in the end, gain him respect and enabled him to return as party leader in the years after the war.
- Labour Party members who opposed the war for whatever reason did not actively campaign against it. Instead, they directed their attention to campaigning for peace and ways in which war in the future could be avoided – and almost all party members could agree with the safeguards that were proposed.
- Arthur Henderson made no attempt to expel party members who were opposed to the war. This helped to heal wounds afterwards.
- Labour Party members who supported the war and those who opposed it were united in their insistence that the material needs of working people had to be protected during wartime and worked together amicably on a variety of committees to ensure that this was so.

Although Arthur Henderson and his colleagues were part of the wartime coalition, they were often uneasy about working closely with men of very different political persuasions. Henderson resigned from the cabinet when he and other Labour leaders were refused permission to attend an international socialist conference to discuss peace conditions. But by this time he and his colleagues were keen to take advantage of party unity and the increasing popularity of Labour in the country at large – helped by the very obvious divisions among the Liberals.

The 1918 constitution and Clause IV

Arthur Henderson's resignation gave him the time and the space to concentrate on creating a new constitution for the Labour Party. His object was to create a party that would weld together trade unionists and working people who were not members of a trade union – and women, who were shortly to get the vote. These were the main terms of the new constitution:

- Local Labour parties would be open to individual members. (In the past, only affiliated groups could join.)
- Membership of the National Executive Committee (NEC) was increased to 20. This would comprise eleven trade union members, five from local parties, four women and a treasurer.
- The NEC would be elected annually at the Labour Party's yearly conference.
- A commitment to socialism was made in Clause IV:

> *The Labour Party's object is to secure for the workers by hand or by brain the full fruits of their industry and the most equitable distribution thereof that it may be possible upon the basis of common ownership of the means of production, distribution and exchange, and the best obtainable system of popular administration and control of each industry and service.*

Read one way, Clause IV could be taken to mean that the Labour Party was committed to the nationalisation of all Britain's industry and services. It could mean the end of private ownership. But the clause, when read closely, is remarkably vague. It is probable that Henderson designed it deliberately to create a programme that was clearly different from the Liberal and Conservative programmes, that offered an alternative to the type of socialism emerging in Bolshevik Russia, but which at the same time was vague enough for all party members to unite under it.

In June 1918, the party conference adopted a programme for future policy development that had been drawn up by Sidney Webb, who had worked with Arthur Henderson on the new constitution. The four main elements in the programme, which formed the basis of Labour Party policy for many years to come, were:

- a minimum acceptable working wage and a standard 48-hour working week

- democratic control of industry, including the nationalisation of key industries
- heavier taxes on high incomes to fund social services
- surplus wealth to be used for the common good, defined as educational and cultural improvements for the benefit of all.

THE FIRST LABOUR GOVERNMENT, 1924

In his memoirs, J.R.Clynes, the deputy leader of the Labour Party, wrote:

> *As we stood waiting for His Majesty, amid the gold and crimson of the Palace, I could not help marvelling at the strange turn of fortune's wheel, which had brought MacDonald the starveling clerk, Thomas the engine driver, Henderson the foundry labourer and Clynes the mill hand, to this pinnacle.*

When James Ramsay MacDonald put together a Labour cabinet in 1924, he had one overriding aim: to convince the city institutions, the various departments of state and the general public that Labour was a party fit to govern. After all, it was a new party and untried in power. There were worries and concerns that socialism would bring revolution in the Russian style. MacDonald had to convince the doubters and at the same time give senior members of his party experience of government. If he could do this, no matter for how short a time his administration ran, more votes and seats would be won and Labour, next time, could focus on the reforms it really wanted to introduce. In this, he was helped, ironically, by being a minority government. MacDonald used the fact that Labour was in office but not in power to good effect in controlling the left-wing elements of the Labour Party and in persuading them that it was necessary to follow a moderate line in policy making.

What did the Labour government do?
In many ways, there was no real difference between the Labour administration and the previous Conservative and coalition governments:

- There were minor reforms in the social services: old age pensions and unemployment benefit were both raised.
- State scholarships to universities were revived, undoing the cuts of the 'Geddes axe'.
- A Housing Act increased the subsidies paid to local authorities that resulted in the building of 521,200 new houses in the following ten years.
- There was no real attempt to grapple with the problems of unemployment; MacDonald just kept hoping for a trade revival.
- Industrial unrest continued, showing that MacDonald was certainly not in the pocket of the trade unions:
  - He was ready to use troops to unload ships during a dock workers' strike had the strike continued.
  - He proclaimed a state of national emergency during a London bus and tram strike.

Ramsay MacDonald, acting as Foreign Secretary as well as Prime Minister, had some success in foreign affairs:

- He convened a conference that put together the Dawes Plan (see page 122), bringing stability to Franco-German relations and so to Europe as a whole.
- He spoke at the League of Nations in Geneva, bringing prestige to the new institution, and making clear his commitment to disarmament and collective security.
- He gave diplomatic recognition to the Soviet Union and negotiated a commercial treaty with the Russians, which involved Russia receiving a £30 million loan. In return, Britain would receive compensation from Russia for assets seized during the Bolshevik Revolution of 1917.

This last was by far the most controversial issue and likely to end the life of the government when it was debated in Parliament. However, a much more trivial matter brought about the government's fall.

The Campbell case

In July 1924, J.R. Campbell, the temporary editor of the *Workers' Weekly*, allowed the publication of an article that urged British soldiers not to fire on their fellow workers in a class war. The Attorney-General authorised the director of public prosecutions to prosecute Campbell for incitement to mutiny. Since Campbell was only temporary editor at the time and had an excellent war record, the prosecution was likely to fail. The Attorney-General decided that it would be sufficient if Campbell wrote a letter of apology, and the prosecution was dropped. However, the Conservatives complained that the decision not to prosecute had been politically motivated and the Liberals, scenting blood, demanded the appointment of a committee of enquiry. MacDonald maintained that the government would resign if the Commons voted for such a committee. It did, and the first Labour government came to an end. Asquith said that, never in his 50 years' experience, had he known a government that had 'so wantonly and unnecessarily committed suicide'.

The Zinoviev letter

Although the first Labour government lasted for only nine months, the Labour Party was hopeful of doing well in the forthcoming general election. MacDonald confidently expected to increase the Labour vote and the number of Labour MPs in the Commons. That was, however, before the Zinoviev letter. Four days before the election, the *Daily Mail* published a letter purporting to be from a leading Bolshevik, Zinoviev, to the Communist Party of Great Britain calling for revolution and urging British communists to infiltrate the Labour Party. The letter was used by the Conservatives as part of their election campaign to pour doubt on the loyalty of Labour. Whether it had any effect on the outcome of the election or not, no one will ever know. Certainly, it is now believed that the letter was a hoax, written by a member of the Conservative Party, MI5 or Russian émigrés.

The 1924 election result

Ramsay MacDonald did not return to Parliament, as he had hoped, with an increased majority. He did not return

	Seats won	% vote
Conservatives	419	48.3
Labour	151	33.0
Liberals	40	17.6

Results of 1924 general election

to government at all. But he had good reason to be satisfied with these results. Labour had emerged as the second main political party in Britain.

SUMMARY QUESTIONS

1 Was it the weakness of the Liberals or the strength of socialist and left-wing opinion that created a separate political party for working-class people?

2 Who made the greater contribution to the success of the Labour Party:
Keir Hardie, Ramsay MacDonald or Arthur Henderson?

3 The first Labour government lasted for just nine months. How far, then, can it be judged a success?

4 What were the greatest threats to the Labour Party in 1924?

CHAPTER 13

From Labour to a National Government

It was the Labour Party's tragedy that it won the 1929 general election. Four months after it took office, the Wall Street Crash triggered the worst depression the world had known. Few governments around the world could survive this catastrophe, and the Labour government was not one of them. Its fall took with it the reputation of Ramsay MacDonald, who was expelled from the party he had done more than anyone to build the party from uncertain beginnings to a party of government.

THE DEPRESSION

Why did the Depression happen?

By the 1920s, the USA was the world's most economically powerful nation. Then, in 1929, the US stock market, on Wall Street, collapsed. For various reasons, partly to do with American domestic policies, this financial disaster quickly led to a severe industrial depression in the USA. Determined to retrieve the situation, the US government erected high tariff barriers in order to protect home consumption, and recalled the loans it had made to foreign governments. The immediate effect of this was that world trade collapsed, unemployment rose sharply in all European countries and governments desperately tried to save their people from destitution.

How did the Depression affect Britain?

Britain was one of the first countries to be affected by the USA's collapse:

- The USA was Britain's biggest trading partner. With American markets closed because of the high tariff barriers, there was nowhere for British manufacturers to sell their goods. Some businesses were bankrupted, others had to lay off a large percentage of their workforce. Unemployment, already a problem, soared.

- The income from trade with the USA was the main way in which Britain raised money to repay debts incurred as a result of the 1914–18 war. With the collapse in trade came a huge loss of income and the government could not meet its debt repayments. To make matters worse, the USA called in all the loans made after the war, which meant that it expected its debtors to repay their loans in full immediately.
- Britain was owed money by various of the other First World War allies (Russia, Italy and France, for example) but they were in a similar situation and could not afford to make repayments.
- The situation was exacerbated by Britain going back on to the gold standard in 1925 (see page 122) which didn't make it easy to sell British goods abroad.

The graph gives some idea of the extent of the problem:

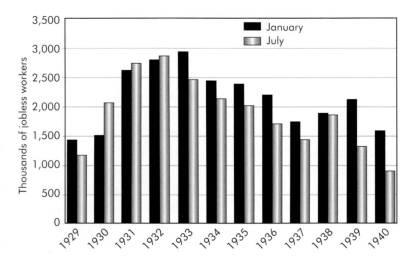

Registered unemployment, 1929–40

Graphs can conceal more than they reveal, as this extract from George Orwell's book, *The Road to Wigan Pier*, written in 1937, indicates:

> When you see the unemployment figures quoted at two millions, it is fatally easy to take this as meaning that two million people are out of work and the rest of the population is comparatively comfortable. This is an enormous underestimate. In the first place, only people shown on unemployment figures are those actually drawing the dole – that is, heads of families. An unemployed man's dependants

do not figure on the list unless they have a separate allowance. A Labour Exchange officer told me that to get at the real number of people living on (not just drawing) the dole you have got to multiply the official figures by something over three.

Shipbuilding	30.6%
Coalmining	25.0%
Shipping	22.3%
Textiles	13.2%
Engineering	8.3%
Chemical trades	7.9%
Skilled building crafts	6.3%
Printing and paper	6.2%
Commerce and finance	3.8%

Unemployment by industry, 1936

And this was far from being the whole story. Unemployment hit different industries in different ways, as can be seen from the table above showing the percentage of unemployed workers in 1936.

Not only were there extreme differences between industries, but there were extreme regional differences as well, as shown in the table below giving unemployment by region.

It is clear that the Depression hit the staple industries – iron and steel, coal, shipbuilding and textiles – the hardest. These industries were located in Yorkshire and Lancashire, the north-east of England, Scotland, Wales and Northern Ireland. By contrast, the service industries, mainly located

Wales	28.5%
Northern Ireland	23%
Scotland	18%
NE England	16.6%
NW England	16.2%
Midlands	9.4%
SW England	7.8%
London	6.5%
SE England	5.6%

Unemployment by region, 1936

in the southern half of England, had relatively little unemployment. Indeed, the new, light industries that had developed in the Midlands and south in the 1920s continued to prosper. Four-fifths of the factories built between 1932 and 1937 were in Greater London.

What were living standards like during the Depression?

A common image of the Depression is of smokeless chimneys, listless people, blackened and miserable terraces of cheerless houses where life was one long struggle against poverty. This was certainly true for some areas of Britain and for millions of men, women and children living there who remained forever scarred by the privations of those years.

But this was not the picture in the whole of Britain:

- At no time in the 1920s and 1930s did retail prices or the cost of living move ahead of wages, indicating that

KEY CONCEPT

Real wages The purchasing power of people's earnings when set against prices. If prices are high, wages buy less. If prices are low, the same level of wages buy more. If wages go up faster than prices, there is an increase in real wages. If prices go up faster than wages, there is a drop in real wages.

purchasing power was maintained even when wages appeared to fall. This meant that **real wages** increased. So the standard of living was maintained and even improved for those in work.

- Expanding sales of consumer goods marked this period, as did access to popular entertainment. More and more people went to the cinema, watched professional sport, read tabloid newspapers and magazines and listened to radio programmes than had done in the 1920s. Cinema audiences, for example, grew from 36,000 a year in 1924 to 8 million in 1935.

- There was an upsurge in the building industry in the years from 1932, when around 1 million council houses were provided at low rent by local authorities as well as 2.5 million homes for the private market. Because construction was a labour-intensive industry, this boom created thousands of new jobs as well as creating a demand for associated products.

Against this background of privation and semi-prosperity, declining staple industry and growing light industry, profound regional differences and attitudes as well as the collapse of world trade and financial markets, how was a government to cope?

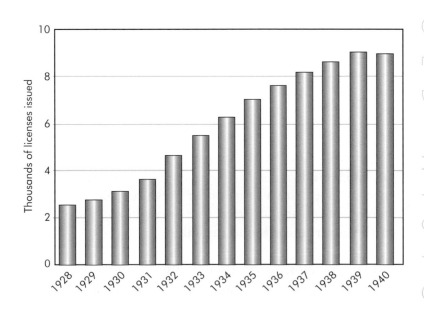

TV and radio licences purchased, 1928–40

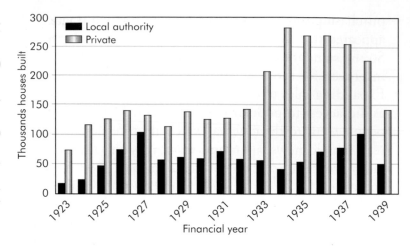

House building,
1923–39

THE SECOND LABOUR GOVERNMENT, 1929–31

In 1929, Labour returned to power, still without an overall
majority and still dependent on Liberal support – but a
good deal stronger than it had been in 1924. Ramsay
MacDonald became Prime Minister for the second time in
his career. He was optimistic: unemployment had dipped
and this would be a good opportunity to gain more
experience of government, to remove the last lingering
doubts about Labour's motives and to win over more
voters so that 'next time' Labour would have an overall
majority. He even appointed Britain's first woman cabinet
minister – Margaret Bondfield, who became Minister of
Labour. But disaster lay just around the corner.

Party	Votes	%	Seats
Conservative	8,656,473	38.2	260
Labour	8,389,512	37.1	288
Liberal	5,308,510	23.4	59

General election results,
1929

The 1931 crisis
During 1931, Britain came under pressure from two
different, but related quarters that created huge problems
that the government found insoluble:

- Foreign investors, frightened by the collapse of the giant
  Viennese bank, the Credit Anstalt, began making

withdrawals from London banks. Between 15 July and 7 August £33 million in gold and £33 million in foreign exchange was withdrawn from London – almost one-quarter of the reserves. The bank rate was raised from 3.5 to 4.5 per cent and a loan was negotiated from France and the USA. But this was not enough to bring back confidence in sterling as a stable currency.

KEY CONCEPT

Balancing the budget
Governments work out budgets every year. In doing so, they must make sure that government expenditure in the forthcoming year will be balanced by the income the government expects to receive.

- **Balancing the annual budget** was proving difficult, if not impossible. Increasing unemployment meant that more and more had to be paid out in benefits. Fewer people in work meant less being paid to the government in taxes. The only way to get the budget to balance was to reduce government expenditure, increase taxation, or both.

It was over the second problem – balancing the budget – that matters came to a head. The Chancellor of the Exchequer, Philip Snowden, was forced by pressure from the Liberals to set up a committee to suggest what could be done.

The May report

On 17 March a committee was appointed, headed by Sir George May, and comprising largely of businessmen and accountants, but with one trades unionist – Alan Pugh of the Iron and Steel Trades Confederation. Its terms of reference were to 'make recommendations to the Chancellor of the Exchequer for effecting forthwith all possible reductions in the national expenditure'. And this is just what the committee did.

On 30 July, the May committee reported. It calculated that £120 million was needed to balance the budget, and it recommended that £23 million should be found from

The May Report's proposals for government spending cuts

Savings on unemployment relief	£67m
Reduction in teachers' salaries	£14m
Reductions in pay to the armed services	£2m
Reductions in police pay	£1m
Postponement of road schemes	£8m
Miscellaneous	£5m

increased taxation, and £97 million by cuts in government spending.

The report was published by the government on 31 July and the cabinet, anxious to go away on holiday, agreed to meet to discuss it on 25 August. But the economic situation worsened and ministers were recalled from their holidays on 19 August.

What did the cabinet decide to do?

The government's preferred policy had been to leave the budget unbalanced for as long as possible, hoping for better times and an upturn in world trade. But this was gradually becoming untenable. The weight of orthodox advice was to make swingeing cuts in government expenditure, but this would mean cuts in social services – probably unemployment benefit – which most of the Labour cabinet would be unwilling to accept. However, the Bank of England was dipping further and further into its gold reserves to buy the pounds of those investors who wished to cash in their investments. International confidence was essential if Britain was to maintain the gold standard – and international confidence could not be maintained for long while the budget remained unbalanced. Snowden was convinced that the only way out of the apparent impasse was to borrow from international bankers. But a condition of the loan would be a balanced budget and this entailed making cuts in government expenditure.

On 19 August, the cabinet was in session for nearly twelve hours, arguing about the extent of cuts in government expenditure, how large they should be and where they should fall:

• Philip Snowden believed that unemployment benefit should be cut by 10 per cent, arguing that this particular benefit could not and should not be maintained at its current rate when all other areas of government expenditure were being slashed. A cut of 10 per cent would, he argued, take the benefit back to the pre-1924 level (when the first Labour government had increased it) and, as prices and the cost of living had fallen, the unemployed would not suffer unduly.

- The economist Maynard Keynes advised the government to think radically and follow an alternative strategy: Britain should come off the gold standard, causing the pound to sink in value. Britain's exports would then become cheaper and competitive and would begin to sell abroad, so lowering the balance of payments deficit and easing the financial crisis. Furthermore, the Bank of England would not need to deplete its reserves of gold to support the pound. The only cabinet member to support this strategy that, with hindsight, was the correct one, was Ernest Bevin.
- Arthur Henderson and his supporters, while agreeing to a raft of reductions in government expenditure, insisted that the unemployed had suffered enough at the hands of capitalism and that to cut their unemployment benefit would victimise them further.
- A delegation from the TUC lent considerable support to Henderson's plea not to touch unemployment benefits.

Ramsay MacDonald did his utmost to bring about consensus. Eventually, the cabinet agreed unanimously to cutbacks totalling £56 million. This was not enough. The key issue remained: should unemployment benefit be cut?

Cabinet records betray the tortured logic of MacDonald's position:

> *A scheme which inflicted reductions and burdens in almost every other direction, but made no appreciable cut in unemployment benefit, would alienate much support and lose the party their moral prestige, which was one of their greatest assets. In conclusion, the Prime Minister said that it must be admitted that the proposals as a whole represented the negation of everything the Labour Party stood for, and yet he was absolutely satisfied that it was necessary, in the national interest, to implement them if the country was to be secured.*

Henderson and his supporters in the cabinet were furious. They insisted that cuts in benefits would be regarded as a betrayal by Labour voters. If the unemployed and workers in general were to face reductions in their standard of living, then the government should resign and another party should impose them.

MacDonald and Henderson each believed the other was betraying Labour ideals. When a vote was taken, the cabinet was divided 11–9 in favour of a complete package of cuts in government expenditure, including unemployment benefit. No government so divided could last, and MacDonald declared his intention of going to the King to offer the government's resignation.

The great betrayal?

Ramsay MacDonald offered his resignation and that of his government to King George V late on Sunday 23 August. The King asked MacDonald to consider forming a National Government. The following day, MacDonald met with the King, Stanley Baldwin who represented the Conservatives and Herbert Samuel of the Liberals. He was assured of their support and agreed to lead an all-party National Government.

On 24 August, MacDonald met his colleagues in what was their final meeting as a Labour cabinet. They were dumbfounded. He was accused of treachery, betrayal and of plotting to retain personal power at the expense of the Labour Party. MacDonald's defence was that he was putting country before party. The Labour Party returned to the opposition benches and, without hesitation, expelled Ramsay MacDonald from the Labour Party.

THE NATIONAL GOVERNMENT, 1931–40

Ramsay MacDonald put together a small cabinet of ten for his new National Government, comprising four Labour, four Conservative and two Liberal members. MacDonald remained as Prime Minister with Philip Snowden as Chancellor of the Exchequer. Stanley Baldwin acted as deputy Prime Minister and Neville Chamberlain was Minister of Health. The Liberal, Herbert Samuel, became Home Secretary.

Getting it right?

One of the first acts of the new government was to implement the cuts to which the Labour cabinet, by a slim majority, had agreed. Snowden's package, which he put before the House of Commons on 10–11 September, comprised

- tax increases of £51.5 million
- cuts in government expenditure:
  - teachers' pay reduced by 15 per cent
  - pay of the armed forces, MPs and judges reduced by 10 per cent
  - police pay reduced by 5 per cent
  - a reduction in unemployment benefits by 10 per cent, a reduction in the time these benefits would be paid, and a reduction of the dole by 10 per cent.

To MacDonald's fury, the Labour Party swung against him and the debate on Snowden's budget became increasingly acrimonious. However, the budget seemed to have done the trick. The Bank of England negotiated a loan of £80 million from New York and Paris, and the pound sterling and the gold standard seemed secure. However, there was trouble brewing. When the sailors of the Atlantic fleet, based at Invergordon, learned that they were facing cuts of 10 per cent while their admirals were having their pay cut by 7 per cent, they refused to put out to sea. News of this 'Invergordon mutiny' was telegraphed round the world and the value of the pound plummeted. This time the government couldn't negotiate any more loans. Britain was forced off the gold standard and the value of the pound slipped even further. However, this meant that British goods could be sold abroad more cheaply: exports were encouraged and imports discouraged. The weaker pound made it easier to balance the budget. Maynard Keynes had been right.

The 1931 election

The government decided to call an election in October in order to get its policies publicly endorsed. The election campaign itself took place in an atmosphere of bitterness and distrust, and most certainly was not fought on issues. MacDonald pointed to the worthless German mark and warned of the dangerous inflation that would ensue if Labour was returned to government and asked for a 'doctor's mandate' to do whatever was necessary; Snowden referred to Labour as 'Bolshevism run mad'. Their former

colleagues responded with accusations of dishonesty and treachery. Baldwin insisted that a vote for the National Government was a vote for 'sound, clean and honourable finance'. The country agreed with him. National Government candidates, 471 of whom were Conservative, won 556 seats. The combined vote for the National Government totalled 14.5 million, whereas the Labour vote fell by 1.5 million to 6.6 million, leaving the Labour Party only 56 seats.

Neville Chamberlain: architect of recovery?

Recovery under the National Government was helped by factors that had little to do with the government itself:

- From the mid-1930s there was a general recovery in world trade. This, along with the weak pound, meant that British goods were cheap to buy abroad. Exports began to rise and this created more jobs.

- Towards the end of the 1930s, all major countries in western Europe were concentrating on armament production – again creating more jobs.
- The National Government was greatly helped by the lack of a strong opposition. The Liberals had been fatally wounded by the split between Asquith and Lloyd George and the Labour Party was still smarting from its self-inflicted wounds of 1931. The general election of 1935 confirmed the National Government in power, although with a reduced majority: the Labour Party was reviving. However, never again in the twentieth century did a government receive over 50 per cent of the popular vote as this National Government achieved.

Neville Chamberlain, who took over as Chancellor of the Exchequer from Philip Snowden in November 1931, built on these advantages:

- He introduced Import Duties, a general tariff barrier of 10 per cent to protect British industry.
- British agriculture was protected from foreign imports. Farmers who produced wheat were guaranteed a minimum price of 10 shillings per hundredweight. By 1939, farmers who produced hops, milk, bacon, oats, barley, meat and potatoes were all protected in the same way. Between 1931 and 1937, the agricultural industry increased its productivity by 15 per cent.
- Low interest rates led to a housing boom, creating jobs and a 'feel good' factor among those able to buy their own home for the first time.
- In 1935, he was able fully to restore public salaries to their pre-1931 levels.

And the unemployed?

The problem of the unemployed remained like a festering sore – painful and refusing to go away. Although unemployment was falling from about 1933 onwards, it remained unacceptably high (see the graph on page 150). For the unemployed, bad times continued:

- The 1934 Unemployment Act set up a national Unemployment Assistance Board which standardised **dole** payments, made when a person's 26 weeks' entitlement to **unemployment benefit** had run out, and paid them using a **means test**. This was fiercely enforced by district officers and deeply unpopular among the unemployed.
- The National Government backed the Iron and Steel Federation, formed in 1932, to supervise the demolition of old, unprofitable works and build new ones, thus creating work.
- The Special Areas Act 1934 applied to regions of high unemployment: South Wales, Tyneside, west Cumberland and southern Scotland. Within these areas, the government financed projects (the steel works at Ebbw Vale, for example). This went some way towards creating new jobs.
- In 1935, the government developed a scheme whereby shipowners could receive government loans to enable them to scrap old ships and buy new ones. This scheme enabled the Cunard–White Star line to order two new liners, the *Queen Mary* and the *Queen Elizabeth*, from the John Brown's shipyard on the Clyde, creating work for unemployed shipyard workers.

Throughout this period, the strongest criticisms came from outside Parliament:

- The British Union of Fascists (BUF) and the British Communist Party, coming from opposite ends of the political spectrum, roundly condemned the government's economic policies.
- The unemployed, desperate when their benefits were cut and they had no prospect of work, protested by going on hunger marches.

Towards the abyss

Ramsay MacDonald handed over to Stanley Baldwin, who won the election of 1935, although with a decreased majority because of an upturn in support for the Labour Party. Baldwin, in turn, retired in 1937 and handed over to Neville Chamberlain. Chamberlain had shown great promise in the fields of social and administrative reform

Unemployment benefit
This was paid out of national insurance and was intended to help working people get through a few weeks, originally a maximum of fifteen, while they found a new job.

The dole This was the money that working people could claim if they had come to the end of their unemployment benefit. It was cut by 10 per cent in 1931 (see page 159) and in 1934 subjected to a strict means test.

Means test Introduced as an emergency measure by the National Government in 1931, this was a 'household test' whereby all income coming into a household was taken into account before benefits were given.

This is a photograph of one of the most famous hunger marches: the Jarrow march. In 1936, the MP for Jarrow, Ellen Wilkinson, organised a march of unemployed men from Jarrow, in the north-east, to London. Their aim was to draw attention to their plight and to present a petition to the King. When they got home, they found that their dole money had been stopped because they had not been available for work – even though there was no work to be had.

and it was here that his talents and his interests lay. However, his administration became preoccupied with the dreadful and terrifying threat that Hitler's aggression was posing to the peace and fragile security in Europe.

SUMMARY QUESTIONS

1 Why did the Depression affect different areas of Britain in different ways?

2 How far could the first Labour government be regarded as a success?

3 The second Labour government was split in 1931 over the question of whether or not to cut unemployment benefits. With whose view, and why, are you most in sympathy: Ramsay MacDonald's or Arthur Henderson's?

4 Ramsay MacDonald's actions in ending the second Labour government and establishing the National Government has been called the 'great betrayal'. Do you agree?

This cartoon was published in the *Daily Express* in 1936

'Work at last'

5 Study the poster 'Smokeless chimneys'.
  (a) How is the National Government seeking to appeal to the electorate?
  (b) Did the National Government deliver what it was promising in this poster?

6 Study the cartoon 'Work at Last'.
  (a) What point is the cartoonist making?
  (b) Do you agree with him?

AS ASSESSMENT: BRITAIN, 1890–1939

There are many different kinds of questions you can be asked about Britain 1890–1939, and the difference doesn't only come from the content. There are some golden rules you should always follow, no matter what the question:

- **Read the question carefully.** Make sure you know what the examiner is asking you to do.
- **Work out** how the examiner is expecting you to use any source material attached to the question. Are the sources there to test your skills of evaluation? Are they there to act as a stimulus? Are you expected to combine the sources with your own knowledge?
- **Look carefully** at the question stems. 'Explain …', 'Describe …', 'How significant was…?', 'Compare …' are all asking you to do different sorts of things with the knowledge you have about a topic. It is NEVER possible to have a general essay in mind about a topic, and to use it no matter what the main thrust of the question.
- **Make sure** you have a sound knowledge base from which to work. Remember that in a two-part question, you should know enough about both parts to have a chance of a successful answer. Examiners can never give you more marks than the total printed on the examination paper, no matter how brilliant your answer. Marks cannot be moved around between the different part-questions.
- **Consider** the number of marks allocated to the question. This will give you a clue as to the length of answer the examiner is expecting. A two-part question with a mark tariff of, say, 10 and 20 will be expecting candidates to write roughly half as much for the first part of the answer as for the second.
- **Plan your essay before you write.** Time spent doing this is NEVER wasted. Planning will enable you to use relevant material to answer the question, develop an argument and, where appropriate, use the source material properly.

ESSAY QUESTIONS

Question 1 in the style of AQA

How effective was the legislation of the Liberal governments from 1905 to 1915 in tackling poverty in Britain? (30)

Reading
You will need to read Chapter 2.

How to answer this question
The question is asking you to analyse the effectiveness of legislation in dealing with poverty. The emphasis is on 'effectiveness' and you need to produce an argument that focuses on this.

Plan
You must plan your essay in order to avoid simply writing a narrative account of the Liberal welfare legislation and to make sure you focus on an argument about 'effectiveness'.

Your plan could approach the subject thematically and would look like this:

- **Introduction**, in which you set out clearly the direction in which your answer will go.
- **Consideration of the various ways** in which the Liberal governments took, or tried to take, various different groups out of poverty. These groups should be children, the elderly, the sick and infirm, and the unemployed. In describing what was done, consider the effectiveness of the measures. Who was left out? Who did not qualify? Who was helped? You could, too, consider whether the causes or the symptoms of poverty were addressed.
- **Consideration of the different interpretations** of the effectiveness of the welfare reforms, and the importance of the beginnings of limited state intervention.
- **Balanced, supported conclusion** about the overall effectiveness of the Liberal legislation in tackling poverty, relating this back to the findings of Booth and Rowntree.

Question 2 in the style of AQA

> Why was partition decided upon as the 'solution' to the Irish question in 1921?
>
> (30)

Reading
You will need to read Chapter 9.

How to answer this question
This is a causation question, which means you will need to focus on 'why' partition happened. But it is more than this. You will need to go further and consider why politicians believed that partition was the solution to the Irish Question.

Plan

You must plan your essay in order to avoid simply writing a narrative account about the events leading to partition and to make sure you focus beyond the reasons for partition on the reasons why politicians thought partition was the only solution.

Your plan might look like this:

- **Introduction**, in which you outline the main steps that took Britain and Ireland towards partition.
- **Consideration of the reasons why** the various politicians involved (British and Irish) believed that partition was the only solution. Avoid taking each politician in turn, but take the reasons in turn and discuss in what ways they were attractive to the various politicians.
- **Consideration of the different interpretations** about the reasons for partition.
- **Supported conclusion** in which you give a direct, succinct answer to the question, showing how you reached your judgement. Aim to show the examiners that you can prioritise, and that you can support any judgement you make.

Question 3 in the style of OCR

> (a) How do you explain Lloyd George's fall from power in 1922? (30)
> (b) Compare the importance of the main causes of the General Strike in 1926. (60)

Reading

You will need to read Chapters 7 and 10, and use the index to pick up references to Lloyd George in other chapters that might indicate where he alienated individuals and/or factions and interest groups. You will also need to read Chapter 11.

How to answer this question

This is a two-part question, with the (b) part worth twice as many marks as the (a) part. This means you should aim to spend twice as long answering the (b) part. Remember, no matter how brilliant your answer to (a), it cannot score more than 30 marks. Examiners are not allowed to transfer marks between part-questions.

(a) This part-question is asking for an explanation of an event. It is, however, asking you to go beyond the actual event in 1922 and to look at the variety of reasons that led up to that event.

Plan

You must plan your answer to the first part-question in order to avoid writing a narrative account of the events of 1922 and to make sure you focus on the long-term as well as the short-term reasons for Lloyd George's fall from power.

Your plan might look like this:

- **Short, snappy introduction**, focusing on what happened in 1922, making it clear to the examiner that you mean to go beyond this to consider in-depth short-and long-term causes.
- **Focus on the Asquith/Lloyd George split** and the way in which this developed into an irreconcilable rift between the two men, leaving Lloyd George clinging on to power at the head of a Conservative-dominated government, while Asquith led the rump of the Liberal Party into opposition. Again, avoid narrative and try to focus on the power struggle itself, looking at the power base of both men and the ways in which this shifted.
- **Discussion of the attraction, to the parliamentary Liberal Party and to the electorate, of each man**, showing how it was that Lloyd George could not depend on a personal following in Parliament and the country. Here you could bring in such matters as his challenge to the House of Lords and his sale of offices.
- **Conclusion**, giving a direct answer to the question, giving a considered, balanced explanation of why Lloyd George fell from power in 1922.

(b) This part-question is asking you to compare the main causes of the General Strike of 1926. You need to use you own knowledge to decide which were the main causes of the General Strike and then consider their relative importance.

Plan

You must plan your answer to this second part-question in order to avoid writing a narrative account of the causes of the General Strike and to make sure you focus on a comparison of the importance of the causes you have chosen.

Your plan might look like this:

- **Brief introduction**, setting out the range of causes that together brought about the General Strike.
- **Sharp focus on the central causes**, comparing the importance of each of your selected causes. Try to avoid describing each cause in turn, but rather write about their importance and the way they interact.
- **Clearly argued conclusion**, in which you show that you can prioritise the causes of the General Strike.

Source-based question in the style of Edexcel: using a source as stimulus

Source 1
From Wal Hannington, *The Problem of the Distressed Areas* (1937)

The worst effects of the slump have been felt in four of the basic industries of this country – namely coal, iron and steel, shipbuilding and textiles. The unemployment which has affected these industries is not an unemployment occasioned by seasonal conditions in the whims and fancies of fashion, as might be said by certain other minor trades. There is evidence of the very big breakdown of the capitalist order of society when the basic industries of the system are plunged into continuous slump; when the mines are sealed up and allowed to become flooded; when steel works are allowed to rust and crumble; when special companies are formed to undertake the task of dismantling and breaking up shipyards; and millions of valuable textile spindles are turned into scrap metal.

(a) Study Source 1. What, according to Source 1, is Wal Hannington's assessment of the scale of the slump? (10)

(b) Use your own knowledge. Why was the coal industry so depressed throughout most of the 1920s? (14)

(c) Use your own knowledge. 'Nothing but economic depression and dole queues.' How far do you agree with this view of life in Britain in the 1930s? (36)

Reading
You will need to read Chapters 11 and 13.

How to answer this question
This is a three-part question in which the source is used as a stimulus only. You must take careful note of the mark tariffs for each part-question in order to judge how much time you to spend on each part.

(a) This is a straightforward comprehension question with a low tariff. Do not, therefore, spend a lot of time planning or answering it. Remember, though, that you are not being asked for your assessment of the extent of the slump, but Wal Harrington's. Examiners will expect you to show an understanding that Harrington believed the slump hit Britian's basic industries in a way that was different from the usual sort of seasonal slumps, and that the basis of his attitude was that he thought capitalism had collapsed. Back up what you say with short quotations from the source.

(b) Again, compared to the (c) question, this part-question has a relatively low tariff. Don't spend time making a detailed plan – just jot down the main points you want to make and then start writing your answer. Some of the reasons you might want to include would be the world surplus of coal; the inefficiency of many British mines; Britain's return to the gold standard; the Dawes Plan and new technologies such as hydro-electric power and oil-fired turbines. You will gain top marks if you can show the links between the reasons you give and the link to unemployment.

(c) This is the high tariff question and you should plan your answer carefully. You should aim to argue that the view of Britain given in the quotation is true of only part of Britain, and the bulk of your answer should be devoted to showing how there were great regional differences in Britain of the 1930s. Back up what you say with carefully selected examples. Beware of simply describing these differences. Aim to show the examiner that you understand why these differences existed and how they changed as the 1930s progressed, with rearmament bringing about a revival in the 'old' industries of iron, steel and coal. Remember that the question is asking you 'how far' you agree with a particular view, so you must aim to come to a balanced, supported judgement.

To what extent was the First World War responsible for the longer-term Liberal decline?

The First World War undoubtedly created a watershed in the fortunes of the Liberal Party. This one cataclysmic event turned British politics upside down and affected every man, woman and child (electors and potential electors) in the country. The Liberal party went into the war as the party of government and it would be unrealistic to expect them to have emerged unscathed and unchanged in 1918. At the very least, the First World War:

- created a crisis of conscience and confidence for Liberals wedded to ideals of individual freedom and laissez-faire
- made a rift between these 'old' Liberals and the 'new' Liberals like David Lloyd George
- brought about the Asquith / Lloyd George division that split the Liberal Party
- necessitated a coalition that gave the Conservatives a route back into power and Labour MPs practice in government
- changed social attitudes amongst the electorate and potential electorate.

But, were changes in Liberal fortunes discernible before 1914? Was it merely a matter of time before they were squeezed out by the up-and-coming Labour party? Or were the Liberals actually in the process of evolving as a progressive party, led by professional politicians and intellectuals intent on synthesising Liberalism with socialism?

BEGINNING TO CHANGE THE PATTERN?

The 1906 general election saw the overwhelming defeat of the Conservatives and this was due in no small part to the ability of Liberals and the Labour Representation Committee to mobilise votes and increase turnout by eight per cent.

There was clearly a very strong anti-Conservative vote.

- Many thousands of Conservative voters converted to Liberalism in opposition to tariff reform.

- In constituencies in London, Lancashire, north-east England and Scotland, Conservative defections were more important than increased turnout in explaining Conservative losses.
- The presence of Labour candidates, particularly in some industrial areas, attracted the working class anti-Conservative vote.
- Many of the 'villa-Tories' of the Home Counties, upset by the 1902 Education Act, turned to the Liberal Party.
- Many Conservatives, unable to support Balfour yet unwilling to vote Liberal, simply abstained.

An anti-Conservative vote however, whilst going some large way to explaining the 1906 Liberal landslide, could only deliver short-term advantages to the Liberals. Disaffections on single issues rarely last and voters revert to type. Although the 1906 Liberal landslide was clearly increased by former Conservative voters influenced by such issues as tariffs and education, their support could not be expected to be maintained in the years before 1914. This support had, in fact, fallen away by the 1910 elections, when the Liberals lost many of their newly gained seats in southern and county constituencies. However, the Liberals maintained themselves in power, despite the withdrawal of this middle-class support, because of their retention of the working-class vote. Indeed, in 1910 the Liberals were still gaining working-class seats from the Conservatives in the north and in London. It can be argued that 1910 provided corroboration that 1906 was not a freak result. It was part of a longer-term change. The Liberal Party seemed to be adapting to the needs of an emerging, politically self-conscious working class. Old age pensions, national insurance, the Children's Charter, the Trades Board Act and the Trades Disputes Act all provide evidence for this.

On the other hand, it is possible to argue that the Liberal party was, by 1914, losing its grip on the electorate. After 1910, the Liberal government was reliant on the Irish and the Labour vote to stay in power. It was facing an unprecedented wave of strikes between 1910 and 1914; 1912 alone saw over 41 million working days lost. Ireland was on the verge of civil war and the suffragettes were more than a minor irritant. The trades unions were adamantly opposed to national insurance, and regarded much of the Liberal's social welfare programme as a 'bosses charter' that ignored their real needs like a minimum wage, improved working and living conditions and the right to work. But, these are mere straws in the wind. By 1914, the parliamentary Liberal Party was very much in control and looking forward confidently to electoral victory in 1915.

It is possible, as historians like Martin Pugh have determined, to detect a shift at this time from traditional nineteenth century voting patterns, that were based on community and religious affiliation, to a twentieth century pattern based on class. In the years before 1914, it seems that it was by no means certain that the working-class vote would go to Labour. Neither was it certain that Labour would emerge as a party of government.

WHAT WAS THE NATURE OF THE LABOUR CHALLENGE BEFORE 1914?

In 1906, Labour won 29 seats in the Commons. However, 24 of these seats were won in the absence of a Liberal candidate as a result of the Lib-Lab pact. A potential worry for the Liberals was the loss to Labour of their seats at Jarrow and Colne Valley in two 1907 by-elections, and there were some fears that this was to be the shape of things to come. The affiliation of the Miners' Federation to Labour in 1909 took with it 45 Lib-Lab MPs, and a loss of eight seats together with a gain of three left the Labour Party with 40 MPs in January 1910.

The 1910 elections deserve particular attention because they:

- mark the ending of the anti-Conservative support for the Liberals
- show the Liberals as standing for election on the basis of their own track-record
- demonstrate the effectiveness of the Labour challenge.

The Lib-Lab pact seemed to work even more effectively in 1910 than in 1906. Labour candidates adopted all the Liberal policies, and the Liberal organisation worked to get them elected. Within the pact, Labour appeared to do well: 40 seats were won in January and 42 in December. Where the pact did not run, however, there was a very different picture. Labour did not win a single seat in either of the two 1910 elections in the 35 constituencies where there was a three-cornered contest. Its candidates came second in six constituencies and third in 29. Additionally, the Liberals won back Jarrow and Colne Valley, lost to Labour in by-elections, and recovered Gateshead, 'lost' in the Miners' Federation affiliation to Labour. Voters were happy to elect Labour MPs where there was no radical alternative, but where there was the Liberal Party became their party of choice.

But, what of by-elections? Traditionally offering voters the chance to register disapproval of government policies by electing protest or maverick candidates, it might be expected that by-elections would see the return of Labour candidates as a warning shot across the bows of a complacent government. Not a bit of it. Even in industrial areas, where opposition to the government's National Insurance legislation and severe industrial unrest should have seen Labour MPs returned in place of Liberals, Labour failed to win any of the fourteen seats that it contested between 1910 and

1914. There were certainly no grounds for supposing that, had it not been for the intervention of the 1914-18 war, Labour would have taken over from the Liberals as the party of government.

WAS THERE A LARGE POOL OF LABOUR SUPPORT EXCLUDED FROM THE VOTE?

It may be that simply looking at voting patterns is to take too narrow a view of political dynamics in the years leading up to 1914. Roughly four in every ten men (and, of course, all women) were excluded from voting before the First World War. The 1918 Representation of the People Act enfranchised 95 per cent of the adult male population and 40 per cent of women. It can be argued that the social changes brought about by the war, which contributed to the passing of the Act, were directly responsible for the creation of an electorate prepared to vote Labour. However, this argument can only hold good if there was a large pool of disenfranchised potential Labour voters prior to 1918.

WHO WAS DISENFRANCHISED BEFORE 1918?

There were specific, legal disenfranchisements. No man in receipt of poor relief, for example, could vote and neither could men who rented rooms of less than £10 annual value. Those living with their parents couldn't qualify as householders and so couldn't vote, and servants and soldiers living in barracks were disenfranchised, too. So were all women. There were also those who were not legally disenfranchised, but who dipped in and out of the electoral registers as their circumstances dictated. The registration process was complicated and the residence requirement temporarily deprived many, particularly those who moved house frequently, from registering as a householder or lodger.

Would the disenfranchised be likely to vote Labour?
- Domestic servants and soldiers were traditionally regarded by all parties as potential Conservative voters.
- Most men qualified to vote because they were householders, and became householders on marriage. Middle-class young men tended to delay marriage because they were training for the professions or the family business, and lived at home with their parents. They would not be likely, when enfranchised, to vote Labour.
- Those who moved frequently between rented accommodation and occasional periods of time in the workhouse would be unlikely to have any interest in, or affiliation to, any one political party.
- The poor Irish vote, where men qualified, usually went to the Liberal Party because of their commitment to Home Rule.

- Confidential reports to the Liberal Chief Whip in 1911 indicated that a switch to one-man, one-vote would advantage the Liberals. However, in areas where there was a strong, skilled working-class workforce that was heavily politicised, Labour would be advantaged.
- Women remained the great unknown. Many thought, erroneously, that they would vote as their husbands did. The generally accepted belief, however, was that they would vote Conservative.

So it was by no means clear that the Liberal Party was a spent force in 1914. Indeed, there is a strong case for believing that they had been more than partly successful in re-inventing themselves. And so it was with confidence that the parliamentary party and the party in the constituencies prepared for the 1915 general election.

WHO WAS GOING TO WIN?

The 1915 general election was never held because the First World War intervened. But it is possible to make an educated guess as to which party would have won.

- In constituencies where there had been a straight Liberal-Conservative contest in 1910 and a by-election since, the same sort of swings and tendencies were found that had been observed 1906-9 and which resulted in a Liberal victory.
- By 1914, Liberal support in the country at large seemed to have returned to its 1909 level.
- The attempt by the Liberals to abolish plural voting was an attempt to deprive the Conservatives of the advantage this was supposed to bring them. The bill only required its third and final reading when war broke out and the bill was lost. Had there been no war and had the bill become law before the 1915 election, the Liberals would have consolidated their advantage.
- The Liberal 'manifesto' was designed to attract potential Labour voters with its proposals on land-holding, minimum wages and house building, thus giving the Liberal Party a wider appeal than previously.
- Ramsay MacDonald and his colleagues attached enormous importance to Liberal efforts to gain Home Rule for Ireland, which they supported absolutely.

Although it seems unlikely the Liberals would lose a 1915 general election, it is even more improbable that Labour would have won. This means that considerable emphasis must be placed upon the First World War as the vehicle of change as far as the Liberal Party was concerned. They emerged from it broken and divided. So what went wrong?

HOW DID THE WAR CHALLENGE LIBERAL IDEALS?

War was always a challenge to Liberal values and 1914 was no exception. At the beginning of August, with anti-war radicalism strong on the left-wing of the party and with Lloyd George as its potential leader, an immediate split seemed possible. Only after Grey's speech to the Commons on 3 August, did the majority of the party acquiesce to the decision taken by their leaders in Cabinet. Liberals in general and in the parliamentary party in particular, accepted the war with reluctance, determined to compromise their ideals as little as possible. Initially, most were able to swallow the bitter pill. They:

- maintained their belief in economic liberalism by supporting the use of normal commercial routes for procuring military supplies
- accepted interruptions to normal business procedures by holding fast to the hope that the war would be a short one ('over by Christmas')
- held fast to their ideals of a civilised society by supporting the idea that the war was one against brutish Prussian militarism.

This enabled hitherto staunch Liberals to throw themselves into the war effort with fervent enthusiasm. Lord Bryce, for example, chaired a committee investigating German atrocities with very little impartial evidence to hand; C.F.G. Masterman took up government propaganda with enthusiasm; Sir Jesse Herbert worked with the Parliamentary Recruiting Committee, whilst non-conformist clergy up and down the country urged young men to join up.

However, this was out of character for Liberals. Rampant patriotism was considered a Conservative attribute and a wildly patriotic country detracted from Liberalism and enhanced the appeal of the Conservative party. As the war became one of attrition and the whole nation was dragged into the hitherto inconceivable nightmare of total war, Liberal ideals were systematically destroyed. Those Liberals in the country who had opposed their own government began to find Labour a more attractive alternative. Those who had reluctantly supported the war lapsed into an uneasy silence. Liberal ideals and Liberal organisation withered whilst Conservative and Labour gained in strength.

THE FAILURE OF LIBERALISM?

Gradually, the limitations of fighting a war on Liberal principles became obvious in the bloody slaughter on the Western Front. The government faced press criticism, public disillusionment and the demands of a Liberal back-bench ginger group. This ginger group, later to become the Liberal War Committee in 1916, was mirrored by the Conservative Unionist Business Committee. By demanding energy and action, responsibility for military failure was thrown upon the government. Indeed, the ill-fated Dardanelles campaign was very much a hastily thrown together initiative in response to these demands.

Demands for greater energy in prosecuting the war resulted in such illiberal moves as conscription, dilution and a host of government regulations controlling such diverse commodities as pit head coal prices and house rents. The emergency provisions allowed by the Defence of the Realm Act were more and more readily invoked by a beleaguered government, anxious to be seen to be doing something. Politically, this meant increasing support for Lloyd George, always an interventionist, and for his concept of Liberalism. Indeed, Asquith seemed to acknowledge this when he made Lloyd George chairman of a munitions war committee.

Lloyd George's attempts to regulate the munitions industry were part of a larger crisis that saw the failure of the Allied 1915 spring offensive at Neuve Chapelle and Aubers Ridge, blamed by the military on the shortage of shells and, by a process of extension, on general government incompetence. The crisis was compounded by Asquith's denial and Bonar Law's willingness to accept Asquith's statement even though most MPs knew it to be wrong. This further angered members of the back-bench pressure groups. It is thus not surprising that the resignation of Admiral Fisher over the Dardanelles debacle lit the fuse of a crisis that threatened to engulf both the Liberal government and the Conservative leadership. In an effort to avert catastrophe, both Bonar Law and Asquith began on a hasty government reorganisation, more favourable to both of them than allowing the Liberal government to fall and facing the prospect of a general election with an uncertain outcome.

Although Liberal ministers dominated the coalition government announced by Asquith in May 1915, the coalition in many ways represented the failure of Liberalism itself. Britain's lack of preparedness and consequent lack of success in the first months of the war was attributed by many to outdated sentimental Liberal ideals and concepts such as free trade, anti-imperialism and the refusal to implement an effective defence system. Conservatism, with its emphasis on defence, empire and military readiness was seen to be the correct strategy in wartime.

LLOYD GEORGE: THE ANTI-LIBERAL?

Liberalism was seen by many to be further marginalised by Lloyd George himself. His support for military conscription and his readiness to control the domestic workforce were hardly traditional Liberal qualities, destroying as they did the concept to individual liberty. His tentative support of a realignment in domestic politics, implied an almost permanent coalition. Moreover, his embracing of the concept of a 'properly disciplined nation' moved him closer to the Conservatives than to Liberals, even to Liberals faced with the difficulties of total war.

From the middle of 1915, the Liberal party was divided. Lloyd George and his supporters, interventionists, pressed the non-interventionist Asquith and his ministers to introduce conscription. The official Liberal position of voluntary enlistment became untenable from that point. They were forced to maintain, against overwhelming evidence, that voluntary enlistment had not been exhausted. They were seen to be holding out against compulsion whilst admitting that it might have to be introduced, and so were branded as delaying ultimate victory. Asquith was simply reinforcing the image that his heart and his party were not committed to the war effort. Indeed, the Derby scheme was little more than a feeble attempt to deflect the Cabinet crisis of October 1915, in which a clutch of ministers of all persuasions were threatening to resign.

A YEAR OF DISASTER

1916 was a year of disaster for the Liberal Party.

* The war went badly on all Fronts, culminating in the total disaster of the Somme. Here Pals Battalions were wiped out in minutes, bringing the horror of a war (already seen as being mismanaged by the Liberals) to thousands of British families.
* The exclusion of Ireland from conscription, following the Easter Rising in April, demonstrated the tenuous hold the Liberals had on Irish loyalties.
* Repression after the Easter Rising alienated potential Liberal allies, Redmond and the constitutional Irish Parliamentary Party and turned Irish sympathies towards Sinn Fein.
* Resignations from the government, principally those of Carson, Selbourne and Simon, were indicative of dissent and indecision.

DIVIDED LEADERSHIP: DIVIDED LOYALTIES

By November, the agreement of Lloyd George and Bonar Law to form a small war committee heralded the marginalisation of Asquith and a fatal split in the Liberal Party. Backed by threats of resignations, their proposal first had Asquith's support. When this was withdrawn because of his belief that as Prime Minister he should lead any such war committee, compromise became impossible because the intention of Bonar Law and Lloyd George was to exclude him from any involvement in the management of the war. Asquith's resignation on 5 December was a total miscalculation. While Lloyd George offered to serve under either Bonar Law or Arthur Balfour, Asquith angrily refused to serve under anyone and thus unwittingly created the situation in which Lloyd George could become premier. Although most senior Liberals walked with him into the wilderness of opposition, it was Asquith's pride and stubbornness that made him refuse every offer to join Lloyd George's government.

The pressures of the war had set Asquith and Lloyd George on diverging paths and had accentuated pre-war differences between the two men. In wartime, Lloyd George revealed himself as a coalitionist with total faith in a correctly staffed central government. These beliefs were totally at odds with the main tenets of Liberalism. However, it would be wrong to suppose that Lloyd George was the only prominent Liberal to think differently from Asquith. McKenna's 1915 budget, for example, was essentially redistributive and therefore 'liberal' but his move away from free trade most definitely was not.

The idea that Lloyd George was not a Liberal persisted in the Asquithian section of the Liberal party. This, together with his reputation for unscrupulous dealing and exploitation of the press, led to the belief that Lloyd George was a traitor who had betrayed his party for nothing more than naked ambition. A convenient myth.

Political parties tend to recover from splits. The Tories did in 1846 and the Liberals did in 1886. But each time there was only one leader. This time there were two: each with very different agendas and attitudes. One was a prime minister who was not leader of his party. The other was the leader of his party who was not prime minister. Tricky indeed.

CONCLUSION

There can be no doubt that the First World War had a profound effect upon Liberal ideology. The very roots of Liberalism were challenged by the exigencies of total war. But this was temporary: the war ended. Peacetime government returned. Any non-Liberal actions taken by the Liberal government or Liberal-dominated coalition could be seen in this context and dismissed as emergency measures only. Of far more fundamental concern was the split between Asquith and Lloyd George. Conservatives and Labour party MPs were split over the best way to conduct the war, but the Asquith/Lloyd George split went deeper than this. Theirs was a rending of the party over principle and personality which left a legacy of bitterness that could not be papered over in the peacetime world of the 1920s.

Revival and decline: the Liberal Party 1918–29

The years after the First World War were critical ones for the survival of the Liberal party as a party of government. The war had seen the potentially fatal split between Asquith and Lloyd George. It remained to be seen whether the party could re-group and re-design itself with a positive appeal to the new electorate.

HOW WAS THE WAR-TIME COALITION CONTINUED?

December 1918: a hollow victory?

The general election of December 1918 gave a landslide victory to David Lloyd George's coalition – a victory greater than that won by the Liberals in 1906. However, it marked another step in the disintegration of the Liberal party.

- The extension of the franchise and the re-drawing of constituency boundaries as a result of the 1918 Representation of the People Act exacerbated Liberal problems because party organisation in the country was chaotic.
- A large number of prospective Labour MPs had their campaigns run by former Liberals. This was significant enough for comment to be made by both political parties.
- In some constituencies, Coalition Liberals supported Conservatives against Asquithian Liberals, and Asquithian Liberals supported Labour against Coalition Liberals. This was hardly a party presenting a united front to the electorate.
- The strength of the 'victorious' Coalition Liberals was not all it seemed on the surface. The 1918 victory was essentially a victory of the Right and couponed Liberals were successful primarily because there was no Conservative opposition. Indeed, even in areas such as Manchester and Liverpool, uncouponed Conservatives gained easy victories.
- Lloyd George's Coalition Liberals lacked any established power base and, in the Commons, were dependent on the Conservatives.

The Liberals fought the 1918 election as a united party. Unsurprisingly, this illusion of unity was shattered once parliament reassembled. Only 36 uncouponed Liberals survived the rout. They hastily formed the Independent Liberals under the leadership of Asquith, and steadfastly refused to co-operate in any way with the Coalition Liberals. Indeed, they had a small measure of success winning by-elections against the Conservatives in Leyton West, Hull Central and Central Aberdeenshire. However, by the end of 1919, the informal agreement whereby local constituency parties accepted a Liberal from either faction as a prospective candidate had collapsed. The split had become institutionalised, and the unity and strength of the pre-war Liberal party was finally shattered.

Why did fusion fail?

The war had served to strengthen Lloyd George's belief in reform from above. In a post-war world where Britain's power on the world stage and social stability at home seemed threatened, continuing to employ determined government action seemed natural to Lloyd George. Protection of trade and improving health, housing and education demanded state intervention and Lloyd George, regarding himself as a progressive Liberal, didn't see a problem here. Instead, he saw an end to the squabbling of party politics in the creation of a centre party that would fuse the radical wing of the Liberal Party with the radical wing of the Conservatives. This, however, was to be a fusion of those with authoritarian, interventionist views, not a fusion of liberal Conservatives with conservative Liberals.

A 'centre party' committee, comprising coalition Liberals and Conservatives and with Oswald Mosley as its secretary, had existed since May 1919. Churchill and Birkenhead canvassed publicly for a centre party. Lloyd George discussed the idea with leading coalition Liberals and Conservatives and on 6 December 1919 publicly opened his campaign for 'fusion'. Stressing the dangers of Labour and socialism, arguing that a *Labour government would land the country in revolution'*, he privately rejected the idea of being tied too heavily to either coalition Liberals or Conservatives:

> I want a National Party; but I want Liberals in it. I should be quite content if I got such a party by dropping some of the people at both ends who would not agree. I want strong government. I want private enterprise. But private enterprise must give the workers a chance and certainty.

He also wanted, of course, to retain power. However, the rejection of 'fusion' by the coalition Liberals on 16 March and the problems Bonar Law had in selling the idea to the Conservatives signalled its end. They did not, however, end Lloyd George's dream of leading a centre party intent on reconstructing Britain. This end was left to the Liberal (NLF) conference in Leamington Spa in May 1920, where coalition Liberals stupidly claimed to be the true inheritors of the Liberal tradition and were booed off the platform.

Coalitionist Liberal or Independent Liberal?

Coalitionist Liberals and Independent Liberals occupied a strange political no-man's-land. Coalitionists were unable to rejoin their former Liberal colleagues and unwilling to merge their identity with the Conservatives, and so they set about reinventing themselves as a separate political party. Their attempt to set up a network of constituency associations and regional councils, together with a regular journal *The Lloyd George Liberal Magazine*, lacked all substance because grass-root support was lacking from the start. Uncertain themselves, as to what they stood for, the Coalition Liberals were completely unable to convince a disinterested electorate to return them to parliament. Fighting some 25 by-election seats, they lost eight to Labour and only retained the others because of deliberate Conservative support. Liberals were loosing their impact within the coalition government, especially after the 'Geddes Axe'. By 1922, Conservative patience with them and their leader was growing thin.

The Independent Liberals suffered from the same sort of identity crisis. Of what, or from whom, were they independent? What did they stand for? The old, pre-war Liberalism was a spent force. Young and young-ish Liberal radicals were busy joining the Labour Party. There was no one to give a new, fresh impetus to the old Liberal values. Asquith was fast approaching his seventieth birthday and was unable to inject a spirit of purpose into the Independent Liberals. There was no one to challenge the radicalism of Labour under the leadership of Ramsay MacDonald.

DID THE 1922 ELECTION MARK THE DEATH OF THE LIBERAL PARTY?

The 1922 general election was as confused as it was complex. There were four main contestants: the Conservative party, the Labour party and the two Liberal parties. But, who was the defending government party and who was the opposition? Who was fighting whom and over which issues remained far from clear. Local variations and local alliances were frequent, and the electorate was immature and largely untried.

Labour, a united party, fielded an unprecedented 411 candidates and had a radical programme to offer the electorate. Bonar Law, resting in traditional Tory values, was confident of office.

But, what about the Liberals? David Lloyd George had money – the 'Lloyd George Fund' – but no party organisation to support him. His pseudo-radical programme had been hijacked by the Labour Party, rejected by the Tories and despised by the Independent Liberals. He had nowhere to go and neither had his remaining supporters. They put up

162 candidates, only seven of whom challenged a Conservative. The Tories were determined not to let a split vote in 155 constituencies allow in Labour. The Independent Liberals, determined to show themselves as a political party on a national scale, fielded 328 potential MPs. But who were they fighting: Andrew Bonar Law, James Ramsay MacDonald or David Lloyd George? With no clear programme and an inept leader, they stood little chance. The likelihood of a complete Liberal wipe-out was clear for all to see.

The results of the 1922 election were to set the pattern of British politics until the Second World War.

- The anti-Coalitionist stand of Bonar Law was vindicated, making the return of a Lloyd George-style coalition impossible.
- A long period of Conservative domination commenced.
- Labour, with 142 seats, had made a vital electoral breakthrough and outnumbered the combined Liberal party MPs.
- The Coalition (National) Liberals won 62 seats and lost 81, 39 of which were gained by Labour.
- The Independent Liberals ultimately gained 54 seats, but lost heavily in industrial areas to Labour.

The Liberal party was certainly not dead, but it was dying. There seemed to be no possibility of a rapprochement between Lloyd George and Asquith. Both Liberal parties had lost important members. The Coalitionists lost Guest, Addison, Churchill and Greenwood, and of the Independent Liberals, Runciman and Maclean had gone too. They had separately and collectively failed to undercut the leadership, programme and electoral appeal of Ramsay MacDonald and the Labour Party. The Liberals no longer had an effective power base in parliament. Any chance of survival, let alone success, rested on some form of agreement between David Lloyd George and Herbert Asquith.

Unite or die
The differences between Lloyd George and Asquith were personal as well as political. If anything, there was more animosity on the part of Asquith than on that of Lloyd George. Embittered at what he saw as being ousted from the premiership and leading a party he believed had been destroyed by Lloyd George for nothing more than personal ambition, Asquith was adamant that he would never again accept Lloyd George as a colleague. This entrenched viewpoint conveniently forgot Asquith's collusion and mismanagement of government that ended with Lloyd George leading the war-time coalition. It put aside the reality that the 1914–18 war would probably not have been won with Asquith as prime minister and ignored Asquith's role in rejecting rapprochement between himself and Lloyd George. For the moment, the Coalition Liberals would be accepted

back into the 'real' Liberal party, but only on Asquith's terms. For his part, Lloyd George showed no inclination to reject his former Conservative allies and kept tight hold of the Lloyd George Fund. Injection of cash from this fund would have considerably helped the poverty-stricken Asquithian Liberals.

The animosity and mistrust between the two men was reflected in the attitudes of their supporters. Cowdray, a prominent Asquithian, wrote to Vivien Philips, his Chief Whip:

> While my opinion is all for reunion, I consider, if reunion involved in any way our acceptance of Lloyd George, that we cannot afford to pay such a price.

Despite a desire for reunion in the constituencies and amongst many MPs, Asquith and his inner circle continued giving lip-service to unity whilst doing little to bring it about. Lloyd George, meanwhile, was touring the country making rousing speeches urging reunion and a new sort of Liberalism that would challenge the orthodoxies of Labour and Conservatives. This was, of course, nothing more than a bid for power within what he hoped would be a revitalised party.

Squabbles and divisions amongst Liberal politicians of whatever persuasion did nothing for the image of the party. They suffered a loss of seats in a series of by-elections in 1922–23, collapsing in the face of the Labour onslaught in the large industrial cities. Against this background we must regard with some cynicism, Lloyd George's disingenuous comment that:

> If we do not reunite, Liberalism is done for as a national driving force. For that reason I have welcomed every proposal for reunion put forward by Liberals of both sections, and I do not see what more I can do.

What more, indeed, was to be done?

Enter Stanley Baldwin

Salvation for the Liberal Party was to come in the unlikely form of Stanley Baldwin. Andrew Bonar Law's illness and resignation in May 1923 led to Baldwin, the former Chancellor of the Exchequer, assuming the premiership. Facing an economic crisis of profound proportions, Baldwin decided on a policy of protection and sought a mandate from the country by way of endorsement. Here was something against which the Liberals, traditional free-traders, could unite. On 13 November a formal reconciliation was announced, cracks were papered over and the Liberals prepared to fight an election on the single issue of free trade.

Lloyd George released £90,000 from the Lloyd George fund to help fund the election, and 454 potential Liberal MPs prepared for victory.

Was this really the beginning of the way back, or a desperate rear-guard action? Bear in mind the following:

• Reunion had been brought about from outside the Liberal parties not from within and because fundamental differences had not been resolved, reunion was only likely to be temporary.
• The Liberals were essentially fighting on a free-trade platform in a country where free-trade was the current norm. They were fighting for the status-quo, whereas the Conservatives were offering a solution to the country's economic problems.
• Although the Liberals put up 454 candidates, the Conservatives fielded 536 and the Labour Party, 434.

One hundred and fifty nine Liberal MPs were returned to parliament, gaining their seats largely at the expense of the Conservatives who won 258 seats despite a loss of 100. The Liberals remained very much the second party to the Conservatives in rural areas, but it was in the industrial cities that they were completely outdone by the Labour party. Selectively targeting 'winnable' seats, Labour ended up with 191 seats and so became the second largest parliamentary party. The Liberals were pushed into third place – a position from which they have struggled to recover ever since.

The Liberal chief whip reckoned that, of the 159 Liberal MPs, 118 were Asquithians. Lloyd George's followers did badly – nearly half of them, including Churchill, lost their seats. So, it was Asquith's political acumen that was the guiding force behind the decision to join with Labour free-traders in ousting Baldwin's government, and replacing him with Ramsay MacDonald and the first Labour government. But, why did he do this? Could he not have manoeuvred the Liberal party into a position where they might have had a reasonable chance of bidding for power? Probably not. To do this would have meant depending on Conservative support, something neither Asquith not Lloyd George were prepared to do. Baldwin was unwilling, as was the king, to work with any scheme that would keep the Labour party from power. And so the Liberal party, with the strong support of their members in the country at large, brought in the first Labour administration.

DEATH AT THE HANDS OF THE LABOUR PARTY?

The Labour party was hardly in a strong parliamentary position, and it might have been reasonable to expect them to rely heavily on Liberal support, even to the extent of adopting some Liberal policies. Indeed, the strategy of Asquith and Lloyd George in keeping the Liberal party alive depended upon it. This was an horrendous miscalculation.

- Ever since the coupon election of 1918, Labour Party managers had realised that their only hope lay in presenting themselves as an alternative to the Conservatives, not as an alternative government to the Liberals. This meant Labour had to do all it could to annihilate the Liberal Party.
- Ramsay MacDonald had no real hope of continuing his minority administration. He therefore decided to use whatever time he had in power to demonstrate to the electorate that Labour was a responsible party, fit to govern and, most importantly, was independent of both Liberal and Conservative parties.

The Liberal party were thus placed in a no-win situation. They either had to vote for Labour policies whether they agreed with them or not, or vote against them, siding with the Conservatives, bringing the government down and forcing a general election for which they were ill-prepared. This unpleasant situation further divided a demoralised party, with MPs rarely voting the same way in any parliamentary division.

Liberal leadership, organisation and policy

The Liberal party needed desperately to sort itself out. It needed strong leadership in the face of the Labour onslaught, effective organisation in the constituencies and it needed to support many more prospective Liberal MPs. The main ingredient for success here was money – and there was money a-plenty in the Lloyd George Fund. But the fund was Lloyd George's one bargaining counter with the Asquithian 'old-guard' and he held on to it tightly during the first months of the Labour administration. As a result, constituency organisation withered and by-election results showed yet again that Labour was advancing at the expense of the Liberals.

Organisation and leadership however, are not enough for a political party to be successful. The Liberal Party needed a strong, coherent programme that would be attractive to the electorate and sufficiently distinctive for the electorate to make an informed choice between the three parties. It was here that the Liberals had possibly their biggest problem. There was very little to choose between attitudes and approaches of radical Liberals and moderate Labour party members. Asquith had run out of ideas if, indeed, he had ever had any.

In the spring of 1924, Lloyd George took the initiative. His decision to oppose Labour on every possible front ultimately forced a general election. He may well have calculated that without financial support from the Lloyd George Fund, the Liberals would make a poor showing. This could work to his advantage. A small Liberal party, purged of the deadwood of Asquith and his supporters, was one that he could build up and lead into a Liberal future. Pipe dreams indeed. And pipe dreams that totally underestimated the dynamism and appeal of the Labour Party.

The 1924 election

Lloyd George got his election, but hardly on terms favourable to him. Mired in the Labour party's Russian policy, the Campbell case and trounced by the Zinoviev letter, the electorate almost inevitably polarised between radical Labour and the safe hands of the Conservatives. The Liberal message, such as it was, was largely ignored by the electorate and their 340 candidates (hardly a strong showing for a party that still cherished dreams of government) stood little chance of success. The Labour Party, fighting with over 500 candidates, was a match for the Conservatives, confidently fielding 552 prospective MPs.

The Liberals were decimated. Asquith lost his seat and, although Lloyd George was returned to parliament, he was not to lead the small, vigorous party of his dreams. Indeed, it was Labour who were the true victors of 1924. Although a Conservative government swept to power with 412 seats, Labour formed the opposition with 151 MPs. They had soundly and finally swept the Liberals into electoral oblivion.

INTO THE WILDERNESS

The bitter dissent between Asquith and Lloyd George dominated decisions made after 1924. With Asquith in the House of Lords as Lord Oxford, the best that Lloyd George could do in his quest for power was the chairmanship of the Parliamentary Liberal Party. Unable to work within what was left of Liberal Party organisation, Lloyd George slipped back into his pre-war habits of spreading policies through 'expert committees' and 'summer schools'. In the mid-1920s these were funded by the now infamous Lloyd George Fund, to the distress of the financially destitute official Liberal Party. Thus, the development of a new policy and new style cannot be divorced from the struggle for control of the party. Lloyd George, unwilling to commit thousands of 'his' pounds to a moribund party over which he would have little control, inevitably raised the ire and suspicion of a party that needed the Lloyd George Fund in order to become electable. Lloyd George would only make his fund open to the Liberal Party coffers if the Party agreed to support his new pet scheme – a Land League. Was this blackmail or a shrewd political move?

The Land League and agricultural reform

The Land and the Nation, published in October 1925, was the result of private research, funded by the Lloyd George Fund, into the ownership and use of rural land. It argued that private landlordism was unable to produce an efficient and prosperous agricultural industry. It advocated the establishment of a network of local committees to oversee the reforms that were necessary – reforms backed by state help. The following year, disregarding Liberal doubts, Lloyd George set up the 'Land and Nation League' to campaign for his land reform proposals. With some modifications these became official Liberal policy and Asquith and Lloyd George managed some measure of rapprochement.

This was a new and exciting phase for Lloyd George. He was embarking once more on policy making and, in doing so, moving sharply to the left of the political scene. His attacks on the government delighted the Labour party, but he was intent on developing a radical, non-socialist programme, not joining them. He was also intent on taking the Liberal Party with him, supported by his money and with him, of course, as leader.

The General Strike and the ending of a quarrel

The fragile alliance between Asquith and Lloyd George was shattered by the General Strike. Both opposed it and supported Baldwin's government in his actions to end it. But there the similarities ended. Asquith maintained that Britain was facing a profound constitutional crisis and refused to criticise the government in any way. Lloyd George, on the other hand, whilst wanting the strike to end on the government's terms, believed it was essential for him to point out Conservative shortcomings. Asquith, determined to bring matters to a head and force Lloyd George's resignation, totally misjudged the mood of the Party. His own resignation was the outcome.

Lloyd George now had the opportunity he had sought for so long. With Asquith out of the way (he died in 1928) the opportunity was there for a restructuring of the parliamentary party and for massive injections of finance. With successes in by-elections at Southwark and Bosworth, a Liberal revival looked more than possible.

Positive policies

Lloyd George had nailed his colours to the mast two years previously insofar as land reform was concerned. He now turned his attention to the whole economic field. Liberal summer schools, the intellectual hotbed from which most Liberal policies emerged, began to emphasise different aspects of industrial reorganisation. John Maynard Keynes developed his theories on finance and unemployment and, with the support of Lloyd George, headed a Liberal committee of enquiry into Britain's industrial problems. Published as *Britain's Industrial Future* in February 1928, it argued for a vast public works programme and monetary controls in order to stave off the Depression Keynes could see coming.

The 1929 general election

Two more by-election gains (Lancaster and St Ives) seemed to herald a positive future for the Liberal Party. A forthcoming general election would see them more or less united, with the ability to field over 500 candidates and with a raft of fresh, new, radical proposals. Before the election had even been announced, Lloyd George started the campaign by publishing *We can Conquer Unemployment*, a sixpenny pamphlet aimed at popularising Keynes' theories.

The Liberal Party failed spectacularly. Labour polled 288 seats, Conservatives 260 seats and the Liberals a mere handful at 59. Winning seats only in traditional Liberal rural areas, Liberals lost heavily in what had become Labour's industrial heartland, in the north-east, in Lancashire and in east London. They had thrown all their resources behind this election and had been decimated by an electorate clearly deciding between a Labour government and a Conservative one. The Liberals had fought as a third party and were now perceived as one. They could never pull back the industrial working-class voters Labour had made its own. They had totally misjudged the strength, since 1918, of the Labour party and the threat this posed them. Never again would they hold office.

Why, by 1924, had the Liberal Party become the third party in a three-party democracy? An historiographical approach

There can be no doubt that the Liberal Party, in the first decades of the twentieth century, suffered a series of mortal body blows from which it never recovered. From 1900 until the First World War, the Liberal Party regularly polled over 40 per cent of the vote in general elections, and between 1906 and 1915 was the clear party of government. Yet the election of 1923 was the last election in which the newly and, as it happened, temporarily re-united Liberal party polled 30 per cent of the vote and gained 158 seats. In the following year, the Liberals won just 40 seats and were never again to be a major force in British politics.

There can be no argument that the decline of the Liberal Party was rapid and catastrophic. There is, however, a considerable body of argument about why the decline occurred and the exact point at which decline can be detected. Historians agree that the factors involved in the decline of the Liberal Party include the impact of the First World War, the split between Lloyd George and Asquith, the increasing attractiveness of Labour Party policies, growing membership of trade unions and their affiliation to Labour, different leadership styles and the outcomes of the Representation of the People Act 1918. What historians disagree about is the degree of significance that can be placed on these factors and, as a consequence, on the point at which decline can be detected.

TO WHAT EXTENT WAS THE PREWAR LIBERAL PARTY IN DECLINE?

What do the election results show?
It is difficult to argue that the prewar Liberal Party was a political party in electoral decline. Superficially, the figures may seem to suggest this. But, while it is true that in 1910 the Liberals fell from their high achievement of 400 seats in 1906, it is also true that their percentage of actual votes cast, reflecting their popularity among the electorate, did not alter as wildly as the fall in seats may suggest. Certainly, they had no difficulty in remaining the party of government throughout the period because of the support they received from Labour and Irish Nationalist MPs, giving them a majority of more than 100 over the Conservatives.

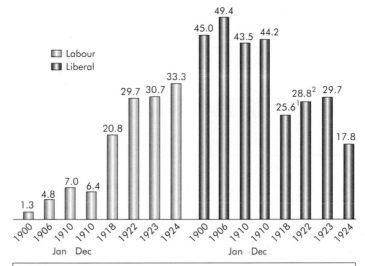

(i) Percentage of votes in general elections 1900–24

Labour
Liberal

1900: 1.3
1906: 4.8
1910 Jan: 7.0
1910 Dec: 6.4
1918: 20.8
1922: 29.7
1923: 30.7
1924: 33.3

1900: 45.0
1906: 49.4
1910 Jan: 43.5
1910 Dec: 44.2
1918: 25.6[1]
1922: 28.8[2]
1923: 29.7
1924: 17.8

NOTES:
[1] 1918: 127 Coalition Liberals won 12.6% of the vote. Official Liberals won 13.0%.
[2] 1922: 53 National Liberals (Lloyd George) won 9.9% of the vote. Official Liberals won 18.9%.

(ii) Number of MPs elected in general elections 1900–24

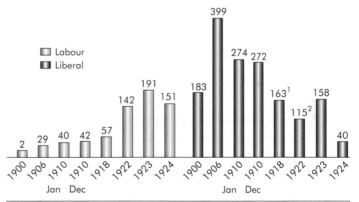

Labour
Liberal

1900: 2
1906: 29
1910 Jan: 40
1910 Dec: 42
1918: 57
1922: 142
1923: 191
1924: 151

1900: 183
1906: 399
1910 Jan: 274
1910 Dec: 272
1918: 163[1]
1922: 115[2]
1923: 158
1924: 40

NOTES:
[1] 1918: 127 Coalition Liberal MPs elected and 36 Official Liberal MPs elected. Total of 163.
[2] 1922: 53 National Liberal (Lloyd George) MPs elected and 62 Official Liberal MPs elected. Total of 115.

Percentage of votes cast in general elections, 1900–24, and MPs elected in the same period

It is true that the Labour Party made some spectacular gains at the expense of the Liberals, but these were mainly because of regional imperatives and were not necessarily indicative of a national trend. They were also due, in no small part, to the Miners' Federation of Great Britain transferring in 1909 its support from the Liberal to the Labour Party. Straws in the wind, maybe, but the Liberal Party did seem able to contain the Labour Party in the general elections and in by-elections up to the outbreak of war.

General election results 1906 to 1914

Party	Jan/Feb 1906 Turnout 83%		Jan/Feb 1910 Turnout 87%		Dec 1910 Turnout 82%	
	No. of seats	% of vote	No. of seats	% of vote	No. of seats	% of vote
Liberal	400	49%	275	44%	272	44%
Cons.	157	43%	273	47%	272	44%
Labour	30	5%	40	7%	42	6%
Irish Nat.	83	0.6%	82	2%	84	3%

What was the nature of the Liberal Party's appeal to the electorate?

It is possible to see the Liberal Party, before 1914, as one that appealed to the electorate on a wide range of issues. It was the party of non-conformity and free trade, Home Rule for Ireland, opposition to privilege, support for the vulnerable and the maintenance of international peace through negotiation. Consequently, the party attracted votes from all sections of society and from all social classes. In particular, the Liberal Party was building up strong support among the industrial working classes, where 'New Liberalism' proved an attractive force which, combined with holding the Labour Party in an informal progressive alliance, drew many into the Liberal fold. **Duncan Tanner** argues this in *Political Change and the Labour Party 1900–18* (1992):

> Before 1914, Labour had not developed the ideological or political strength to support an expansionist strategy. It had not created a solid 'class' vote, based on cultural units which were common to working-class voters. It had not even the uniform support of trade unionists. The assumption that it did is based upon inadequate theory and partial empirical analysis. In reality, electoral politics followed a pattern in which past political and current economic interests combined to create an extremely uneven electoral map. The distribution of support was such that it was comparatively strong where the Liberal Party was weak, and unable to seriously rival it in most Liberal areas. The Labour Party was not on the verge of replacing the Liberals in 1914.

While it is true that the years between 1910 and the outbreak of war were characterised by a series of violent crises relating to industrial strife, Ireland and the suffragettes, it is by no means clear that these indicate a decline in the power and control of the Liberal Party. Liberal MPs were confident that 1915 would deliver them a fourth election victory had the war not intervened. Indeed, **Peter Clarke** in *Lancashire and the New Liberalism*, an important study of pre-1914 Liberalism published in 1971, contends:

The first quarter of the twentieth century saw two sorts of change in British politics. The first sort centred on the emergence of class politics in a stable form; the second sort on the effective replacement of the Liberal Party by the Labour Party. But the first does not in any simple way explain the second. For one thing, the chronology is wrong. By 1910, the change to class politics was substantially complete. That from Liberalism to Labour had not really begun. Nor were there signs that it must begin. It was no light thing to overturn one party and make another to put in its place. At the beginning of the second decade of the twentieth century it looked as if both Labour and Liberalism would be subsumed in progressivism. It seemed that social democracy was bound up with the interests of the Liberal Party.

Did 1910 mark a turning point in the fortunes of the Liberal Party?

The interpretations of the position of the Liberal Party in pre-1914 Britain of Peter Clarke and Duncan Tanner directly contradict the view of **George Dangerfield** who, in 1936, published *The Strange Death of Liberal England*. He argues that the problems faced by the Liberals after 1909/10 were so serious that Liberalism was mortally wounded even before the first shot was fired in the First World War:

The year 1910 is not just a convenient starting point. It is actually a landmark in English history, which stands out against a peculiar background of flame. For it was in 1910 that the fires long smouldering in the English spirit suddenly flared up, so that by the end of 1913 Liberal England was reduced to ashes. From these ashes a new England seems to have emerged. I realise, of course, that the word 'Liberal' will always have a meaning so long as there is one democrat left in the world, or any remnant of a middle class; but the true prewar Liberal England – supported as it still was in 1910, by free trade, a majority in parliament, the ten commandments and the illusion of progress – can never return. It was killed, or it killed itself, in 1913. And a very good thing too.

To some extent, this view is supported by a group of labour historians who dispute the rosy glow put on affairs by academics like Peter Clarke and Duncan Tanner. These historians look beyond the election statistics and claim that there were social and economic forces at work that were undermining the power base of the Liberal government and of the Liberal Party in the country at large:

- **Henry Pelling**, in his essay *Labour and the Downfall of Liberalism*, published in 1968, shows that growing urbanisation coupled with the rising cost of living and economic problems within some industries (notably coalmining) led to an increased class-consciousness among working people that turned them away from Liberalism and toward Labour. He points particularly to the decision of the Miners'

Federation to affiliate to the Labour Party in 1909, thus ending its formal support of the Liberal Party, and to the enormous growth in trade unionism, where membership grew from 2.5 million in 1910 to over 4 million in 1914

- **Roy Gregory**, in *The Miners and British Politics 1906–14*, published in 1968, takes Pelling's point about the miners one stage further. He shows how, by August 1914, the Lib–Lab pact was crumbling on the coalfields owing to differences of opinion between the Liberal coal owners and their socialist union officials.

More recently, historians have claimed that the Liberal Party, prior to 1914, was unable to adapt to the growing demands of a self-aware working class with specific expectations and aspirations. They argue that the Labour Party came into existence to meet these needs, and, as the working class gained greater economic strength through the trade unions, coupled with voting power after 1884 and 1918, the Liberal Party was doomed. Labour was bound to replace it as the political party of choice for the working class.

In his study of the *Evolution of the Labour Party 1910–24*, published in 1974, **Ross McKibbin** claims:

> Labour Party organisation, particularly in the constituencies, was itself only the political side of an industrial organisation that had grown rapidly in the late 19th and early 20th centuries. Almost everywhere the trades councils had become local agencies of the Labour Party.

> Why was it Labour and not the Liberal Party which benefited from these changes? The answer is to be found in the nature of the relationship between the Labour Party and the trade unions on the one hand, and between the trade unions and the industrial working class on the other. Since the Labour Party was inextricably linked with the unions, it, like them, followed the main line of British economic development. Because it had no life apart from the unions, it gained electorally from their growth.

Starting from a consideration of Liberalism and the Liberal Party, **George Bernstein**, in *Liberalism and Liberal Politics in Edwardian England*, published in 1986, reaches a similar conclusion but one based on different evidence:

> Even if there had been no war, the Liberal Party was not in a strong position to retain the support of the working-class electorate in a political world that was moving toward class politics. Liberalism was a set of beliefs which assumed harmony between capital and labour. It was not equipped to defend the interests and redress the grievances of a labour movement which was hostile to capital. There were limits beyond which most Liberals would not go

on issues that really mattered to the workers, like the right to work and a national minimum wage. It should not cause surprise that the Liberals were out of touch with the aspirations of the workers. Both in parliament and in the constituencies, the Liberals were a party of the middle class. If the emergence of class politics meant that the workers wanted a party whose priority was the concerns of the poor and the working class, then they would have to look elsewhere.

Whatever the weight different historians place on evidence and research, there does seem to be a general consensus that there were problems in the Liberal Party's unwillingness to face up to the expectations of an increasingly vocal and united working class. However, the concept of 'class consciousness' is an elusive one and there remains the irrefutable evidence that the electoral statistics show no appreciable shift towards Labour in the period to 1914. **Paul Adelman** sums this up very well in *The Decline of the Liberal Party 1910–31*, published in 1981:

> *In terms of historical analysis, and without underestimating the seriousness of the problems that faced the Liberal government during these years, it is as well to see them in less dramatic and more realistic terms, as problems not essentially different in kind from those that have faced all peacetime governments in this country from Gladstone onwards.*

> *From the electoral point of view it is clear that the Liberal Party was facing serious difficulties before 1914, due more to a resurgence of the Right at both local and national level than to the rise of the Left. But though the Liberals might have lost the next general election if peace had prevailed, especially if the Lib/Lab alliance collapsed, there is little hard evidence that the Liberal Party was dying or even in decline during this period.*

THE RAMPANT OMNIBUS: HOW FAR DID THE FIRST WORLD WAR (1914–18) AFFECT THE FORTUNES OF THE LIBERAL PARTY?

In 1966, a book called *The Downfall of the Liberal Party* by Trevor Wilson was published. In it Wilson says:

> *To make clear the view taken here about when the Liberal Party 'reached the point of no return' it may be permissible to resort to allegory. The Liberal Party may be compared to an individual who, after a period of robust health and great exertions, experiences symptoms of illness (Ireland, labour unrest, the suffragettes). Before a thorough diagnosis can be made, he was involved in an encounter with a rampant omnibus (the First World War) which mounted the pavement and ran him over. After lingering painfully, he expired. A controversy has persisted since as to what killed him. One medical*

An historiographical approach.　　197

school argues that even without the bus, he would soon have died; the intimations of illness were symptoms of a grave disease which would soon have ended his life. Another school goes further and says that the encounter with the bus would not have proved fatal had not the victim's health already been seriously impaired. Neither of these views are accepted here. The evidence of them is insufficient, because the ailment has not yet reached the stage where their ultimate effect could be known. How long, apart from the accident, the victim could have survived, what future (if any) he possessed cannot be said. All that is known is that at one moment he was up and walking, and at the next he was flat on his back, never to rise again; and in the interval he had been run over by a bus. If it is guesswork to say that the bus was mainly responsible for his demise, it is the most warrantable guess that can be made.

So, is Trevor Wilson's analogy correct? Was a fit and active Liberal Party mown down by the rampant omnibus of war? If the Liberal Party was thriving before the war – and we have seen that this is a very big 'if' – then it most certainly was in a very poor state, if not dying, at the end of it. It is a generally held belief that war unites a country behind its political leaders. The problem with this war and those leaders was that it wasn't clear, until the Lloyd George coalition government of 1916, who the real leaders were and where they were leading. And it was the coalition government that brought about the rift between Asquith and Lloyd George that split the Liberal Party throughout the land. If this were not bad enough, the very concept of war and, indeed, its actuality, was anathema to many Liberal consciences.

Did the outbreak of war initiate a process of disintegration in the Liberal Party that reduced it to ruins by 1918? That the Liberal government and party accepted the decision to go to war with little enthusiasm is clear. Two ministers resigned from the government, and a small group of Liberal MPs, resolutely opposed to the war, campaigned for a fair peace, international disarmament and the end of secret diplomacy. The remainder, uneasily, accepted that the party had little choice but to knuckle down and win the war even if this meant acting illiberally. They quickly lost confidence in Asquith as a war leader and threw in their lot with Lloyd George. The rampant omnibus had started to move.

An illiberal home front?

Initially without a strong leader, most Liberal backbenchers reflected the mood of Liberals in the country at large: uneasy and depressed. Forced to face the realities of total war, they had to abandon long-held Liberal principles of free speech and individual freedom and agree to conscription, censorship of the press, the internment of aliens, the doubling of income tax and the Defence of the Realm Act, which gave the government unprecedented powers to act as it thought fit without being answerable to Parliament. Furthermore, Liberals had to watch helpless while the disestablishment of the Church of Wales and Home Rule for Ireland, two measures to which the party was wholeheartedly committed, were shelved indefinitely. Again, it is Trevor Wilson who sums up the situation:

> For a Liberal administration to lead Britain into war and to direct a wartime administration seems almost a contradiction in terms. Its task of international pacification had automatically disappeared. And it had little hope of preserving intact those principles and practices identified with Liberalism: free trade, protection of minorities, the 'pacification' of Ireland, liberty of individuals and voluntary service in the armed forces. Yet once a Liberal government began to modify its ideals under stress of war, how long would it be before the Liberal position was abandoned altogether and that of the Conservatives adopted?

The impact of the split between Asquith and Lloyd George

The anomaly of the Liberal Party running a war, and thus forcing it to be illiberal, was exacerbated by the split between Asquith and Lloyd George. This, indeed, was the central episode that could be said to cause the 'disintegration' detected by Trevor Wilson. The formation of the Lloyd George coalition government in December 1916 with the support of the Conservative and Labour parties undoubtedly won the war but it split the Liberal Party. Herbert Asquith and about half the parliamentary party, including all the former ministers, walked into the wilderness of opposition. Lloyd George's coalition government was therefore dominated by Conservatives, and his war cabinet consisted of one Liberal (himself), three Conservatives (Bonar Law, Milner and Carson) and one member of the Labour Party (Henderson). This informal split did not necessarily have to damage the Liberal Party irrevocably. The exigencies of war could be given as an excuse for the Conservative-dominated war cabinet, and a post-1918 rapprochement was, in theory, possible. But, given the personalities of Asquith and Lloyd George, such a rapprochement was unlikely. In 1917, Asquith refused office in the new coalition:

> Under no circumstances would I serve in a government of which Lloyd George was the head. I had learned by long and close association to mistrust him profoundly

And, although he took reasonable care to avoid criticising Lloyd George through 1917 and much of 1918, the Maurice debate of May 1918 revealed the depth of the differences that divided him from Lloyd George and the extent to which they divided the Liberal Party. The consequences of this were seen in the results of the 1918 election which broke the Liberal Party in Parliament and in the country.

To what extent, though, can the war be seen as the 'rampant omnibus' that destroyed the Liberal Party? The war produced leadership problems and divisions within all three major political parties, but seemingly destroyed only the Liberals. Liberal decline and ultimate destruction cannot be attributed totally to the political impact of the First World War.

HOW SIGNIFICANT WAS THE REPRESENTATION OF THE PEOPLE ACT OF 1918 IN THE DECLINE OF THE LIBERAL PARTY?

The significance of the Representation of the People Act, coming as it did at the end of a war of terrible devastation, voted in by a Parliament rent by schism and with political parties facing an uncertain future, was bound to be profound. At a stroke, the electorate was tripled. What impact would this have on political parties and on the character of future governments?

Enfranchising the disenfranchised.
There was a degree of hidden disenfranchisement in pre-1918 Britain. Women, of course, could not vote in general elections, but there were groups of men who did not have the franchise: paupers, prisoners, living-in-servants and soldiers. Added to this, arcane regulations governing registration and residential qualification meant that an additional 4 million men may have been excluded. By giving the vote to women over 30 and by removing most of the technical difficulties in the way of registration, the electorate leaped from around 7 to 21 million voters. Where would the newly enfranchised place their votes?

The traditional view
An article by **H.G.C. Matthew, R.I. McKibbin and J.A. Kay**, 'The Franchise Factor in the Rise of the Labour Party', published in 1976, argues that the Representation of the People Act was of prime importance in the rise to power of the Labour Party. This argument is based on the assumption that most of the men excluded from the franchise before 1918 were working-class people who would have voted Labour. They calculated that the working class made up about 60 per cent of the prewar electorate; after 1918, this shot up to 80 per cent.

In prewar Britain, the argument goes, support for the Liberal Party came from the middle class and from the élite of the working class. The 20 per cent increase in the working class electorate, people with no tradition of voting at all, was the pool from which the Labour Party drew its support. The argument develops to show that it was the inability of the Liberal Party of the early 1920s to attract this new pool of voters that led to its electoral collapse.

The revisionist view

The assumptions underlying this argument were challenged in the 1980s by the work of **Duncan Tanner** and **Michael Hart**. In *The Parliamentary Electoral System, the 'Fourth' Reform Act and the Rise of Labour in England and Wales* (Tanner) and *The Liberals, the War and the Franchise* (Hart) they show that exclusion from the pre-1918 franchise was a matter of age and marital status, not class. Nearly all householders, regardless of class, were able to get on the electoral register. Those who couldn't were usually young, single males who tended to be mobile, whatever their class, and who in any case had not achieved the status of householder. This would suggest, and Tanner develops this view, that the working-class vote pre-1918 was around 76 per cent and so the rise to 80 per cent was far from as dramatic as had earlier been thought. Even if these newly enfranchised working-class people voted Labour, their influence was in all probability nullified by the influx of women voters (a majority of the new electorate) who voted Conservative or Liberal. Tanner, however, goes on to consider the redistribution clauses in the Act and concludes that many new working-class constituencies were created in London, mining areas and northern industrial towns. It is here that the Labour Party drew its support.

Whatever view is taken of electoral statistics, the central importance of the Representation of the People Act 1918 cannot be denied. It created a large electorate – an electorate that had to be wooed. In the years after 1918, the Liberal and Labour parties fought for the allegiance of this group of voters. The Liberal Party lost. But why?

HOW STRONG WAS THE APPEAL OF THE LABOUR PARTY AFTER 1918?

In 1910, Labour polled about 0.3 million votes. By 1918, Labour was polling 2.3 million and, by 1929, 8.3 million. This steady rise is impressive. By contrast, the Liberal vote fluctuated wildly, and no steady advance from the peak vote of 3 million in 1910 can be detected.

How important was trade union membership?

The problems experienced by the Liberal Party before 1914 in meeting the demands of a growing class-conscious labour force have been discussed earlier in this section. These problems were exacerbated after the First World War, when Liberalism met with a feeling of greater unity among industrial workers and, especially in coalmining, a greater division between capital and labour. The strength of organised labour is seen, too, in the massive increase in trade union membership: from 4 million in 1914 to roughly 8 million in 1918, 75 per cent of whom were in unions affiliated to the TUC. About half the workforce was unionised, making organised labour more powerful in the 1920s than ever before. This provided the Labour Party with a sound and expanding electoral base. Indeed, in the 1918 general election, nearly 200 Labour candidates were sponsored by trade unions. **Paul Adelman** (see above) develops this further, explaining:

> *Owing to the existence of full employment and rising wages during the war, the position of the millions of unskilled workers outside the trade unions had improved enormously, and many of them looked with increasing favour upon Labour's promises to defend their gains, especially through state action.*

What had the Labour Party to offer after 1918?

In the years after the First World War, the Labour Party was able to transform itself into an attractive, electable party for a variety of reasons:

- A secure electoral base developed among the working class.
- The Labour Party constitution of 1918 and associated detailed policy statements spelled out a socialist vision of the future that was immensely attractive to working people, causing Labour Party membership to grow, along with more general support for the party among working people.
- Clause IV gave the trade unions the expectation of the nationalisation of the major British industries – particularly mines and the railways – building on their positive experiences during the First World War.
- The acceptance of Labour politicians into coalition governments on equal terms with Conservatives and Liberals, and in particular Arthur Henderson's participation in the inner war cabinet, gave the Labour Party a prestige and respectability in the eyes of the electorate it would not otherwise have had.
- Labour's focus on policies that were attractive to Liberals – housing and education – and their embracing of disarmament and the League of Nations, drew the more radical Liberals into the Labour Party fold.
- James Ramsay MacDonald was a charismatic leader who was able to express the deeply held feelings of the Labour movement about the needs of the working class.

HOW STRONG WAS THE APPEAL OF THE LIBERAL PARTY AFTER 1918?

The Liberal Party, as will have become clear, was in no position to rival the appeal of Labour:

- The Liberal leaders were in disarray. Asquith was becoming an increasingly remote figure, out of touch with the dynamics of British society in the 1920s. Lloyd George had committed political suicide by his continuance of a Conservative-driven coalition beyond the confines of the war and by his devious industrial policies. There was, quite simply, no one else.

- Lacking dynamic leadership to initiate the development of new policies that were attractive to the electorate, Liberal policies looked outdated and tired. Free trade, Welsh disestablishment and Irish Home Rule had all but disappeared as issues by the early 1920s and the Liberal Party could not, or would not, develop a dynamic industrial policy that would rival that of the Labour Party.
- The social and economic policies of the Asquithian Liberal Party were more mediocre and orthodox than those of Lloyd George (once he had embraced Keynesian economics in his 'coloured books') but there remained the problem of a split party that could not, or would not, speak with one voice.
- Leading Liberals, particularly the Liberal intelligentsia, had no clear ideology to offer as an alternative to socialism.

Thus the Liberal Party drifted into the 1920s as a party of the Right, not the Left. Yet, on the Right the Conservatives were well organised and had a clear ideology and set of policies.

THE END GAME

James Ramsay MacDonald was not just a charismatic leader, adept at voicing the emotion of the working class. He was a skilful political manipulator. He believed that the way forward for Labour was to annihilate the Liberal Party, giving the electorate a clear choice between a party of the Right – the Conservatives – and a party of the Left – the Labour Party. All that Labour had to do was to refuse to engage in any sort of deal with the Liberals, retain the electoral lead it had achieved in 1918, and the British electoral system, never favourable to third parties, would do the rest.

This is exactly what happened. Although dependent on Liberal support throughout Labour's first administration, Ramsay MacDonald steadfastly refused any sort of formal alliance or pact. Lloyd George, caught in a web of his own making, and helpless to influence events, realised what was happening:

> Liberals are to be the oxen to drag the Labour wain over the rough roads of Parliament, and when there is no further use for them, they are to be slaughtered.

And the Liberals were slaughtered in the general election of 1924, never again to achieve power.

WAS THE COLLAPSE OF THE LIBERAL PARTY INEVITABLE?

It is very tempting, when looking at something like the collapse of an administration or a political party, or the rise to dominance of what was once a faction, to assume inevitability. Because it happened, it was inevitable that it should happen. This is nonsense.

Paul Adelman (see above) considers how things could have turned out differently:

> That process [of decline] might not have occurred at all, or might have assumed another form, if different political decisions had been taken by the men involved: if, for example, Asquith had joined Lloyd George's government after 1916; if Lloyd George had supported more resolutely the proposals in favour of proportional representation produced by the Speaker's Conference in 1917; or if the Liberal leaders had behaved more astutely in 1924.

A2 ASSESSMENT: THE DECLINE OF THE LIBERAL PARTY, c.1900–29

SOURCE-BASED QUESTION IN THE STYLE OF EDEXCEL

Edexcel assesses knowledge and understanding of the reasons for the decline of the Liberal Party in Paper 4A of its Unit 6. To be successful, it is essential that you understand the focus of this unit and the target for each of the two questions. This will enable you to organise and deploy your knowledge and skills so that you maximise the marks you can gain.

What is the unit focus?
Edexcel's Unit 6 is a synoptic unit. In it, you are expected to show the full range of skills, concepts and competencies you have gained through studying the other five units. This means that you are expected to

- show how your understanding of such things as bias and reliability help you create an argument, or explanation in answer to the question set
- deploy your knowledge of the period
- demonstrate your understanding of concepts like change and continuity, similarity and difference.

What are the question targets?
(a) making a judgement based on an understanding of a range of historical perspectives, making linked use of own knowledge and sources of different types.
(b) making a judgement about an historical interpretation based on an understanding of a range of historical perspectives, making linked use of own knowledge and sources of different types.

You MUST make sure, when you are answering question (b), that you use the sources to lead your answer. They should be the building blocks around which you construct an argument.

THE DECLINE OF THE LIBERAL PARTY, c.1900–29

Source 1
From a speech made by Winston Churchill on 11 October 1906

The cause of the Liberal Party is the cause of the left out millions. No man can be a collectivist alone or an individualist alone. Collectively, we have an army and a navy and a civil service, we have a post office and a police and a government; collectively, we light our streets and supply ourselves with water; collectively, we indulge in all the necessities of communication. But we do not make love collectively, and the ladies do not marry us collectively, and we do not eat collectively and we do not die collectively and it is not collectively that we face the sorrows and hopes, the winnings and losings of this world of accident and storm. No view of society can be complete which does not comprise within its scope both collective organisation and individual incentive. The very growing complications of civilisation create for us new services which have to be undertaken by the state.

Source 2
From L.T. Hobhouse, *Liberalism* (1911)

It is the function of the state to secure the conditions upon which mind and character may develop themselves. Similarly, we may say now that the state is to secure conditions upon which its citizens are able to win by their own efforts all that is necessary to full civic efficiency. It is not for the state to feed, house and clothe them. It is for the state to take care that the economic conditions are such that the normal man who is not defective in mind or body can by useful labour feed, house and clothe himself and his family. The 'right to work' and the 'right to a living wage' are just as valid as the rights of person and property. Society owes [to the labourer] the means of maintaining a civilised standard of life and this debt is not adequately discharged by leaving him to secure such wages as he can in the haggling of the market.

Source 3
From C.L. Mowat, *Britain between the Wars* (1955)

The greater part [of Liberals] which had followed Lloyd George into the Coalition, had become prisoners of the Conservative majority. The non-Coalition Liberals, with almost all their leaders defeated from Asquith downwards, were a mere rump, and considered disbanding altogether, but held together under the leadership of Sir Donald Maclean. Subsequently, the party recovered a good deal of its strength, and for a time also its unity; but never again was it anywhere near to obtaining a parliamentary majority. Not that the coupon election was more than a milestone on the road of its decline. The split between Asquith and Lloyd George, dating from 1916, was fatal, and it was never healed, in spite of several attempts, particularly in 1918. Even further back, the party had showed mortal weakness, when its formula of discussion and compromise had failed to meet the pre-war tests of the Tory revolt over Ulster, the suffragettes' campaigns, and the great strikes of 1910–13. The rise of the Labour Party had ended its claims to radicalism; and the middle ground which was all that remained to it proved no more than a sand spit.

Source 4
From P. Adelman, *The Decline of the Liberal Party* (1981)

There is evidence that the electoral system which existed before 1918 was far less democratic than previously supposed. Not just women, but large groups of men were excluded and, owing to outdated registration and residential qualifications, many men did not vote. It has been estimated that 40–45% of men in pre-war England did not vote for one reason or another. As a result, the industrial working class did not form the majority of the electorate and the Liberal Party's political power was based, not on a mass electorate but on the support of the middle classes and an élite of workers. This explains the enormous importance of the Representation of the People Act, 1918. The Act trebled the electorate, for the first time making the industrial working class a majority in the electorate. It seems probable that it is from these new voters that Labour drew its electoral strength in the post-war world.

Source 5
From M. Pugh, *The Making of Modern British Politics 1867–1939* (1982)

The traditional view that Edwardian politics was characterised by a Liberal Party too ideologically rigid and rooted in middle-class radicalism to avoid being outflanked by a socialist party or to survive the emergence of a working-class electorate has proved to be virtually untenable. Yet the evidence that has destroyed the old view has also generated an alternative interpretation.

The 'Progressive' interpretation amounts to much more than the view that Liberalism survived the Edwardian elections; it suggests that it adapted to the chief trends of twentieth-century politics, flourishing on the basis of its social-economic appeal to the working class. The implication is that there was nothing inevitable in the rise of Edwardian Labour as a governing party.

The more the Edwardian evidence underlines the fact that the Liberals were in no imminent danger of decline, let alone eclipse, the more importance must, apparently, be attached to the First World War as the decisive factor in their downfall.

Answer both questions (a) and (b)

(a) Using the evidence of Sources 1, 2 and 5, and your own knowledge, how far do you agree that, by 1914, the Liberal Party was flourishing on the basis of its social and economic appeal to the electorate? (20)

How to answer this question
The question is asking you to use the three sources and your own knowledge to make a supported judgement on the state of the Liberal Party in 1914 on the basis of its appeal to the electorate.

- Read the three sources carefully and decide what evidence they give you about the appeal of the Liberal Party by 1914.
- Decide on the status of the evidence. Is it, for example, biased? Is it reliable?

Your own knowledge should be based on Chapters 1, 2, 3, 5 and 6 as well as the A2 Section.

- Decide whether or not you agree that the Liberal Party was flourishing on the basis of its appeal to the electorate. Remember – it's bound to be more complicated that a straightforward 'Yes' or 'No'.
- Plan a line of argument, or series of linked points, that you want to make.

- Select from the sources and from your own knowledge, relevant material to support the points you want to make. Remember to use the evidence of the sources – not simply what they say. If you're confused about the difference between evidence and information, remember that for the former you must ask 'Of what is this source evidence?' and of the latter you must ask 'What does this source tell me?'
- Do not go through the three sources one by one, but aim to use them, separately or together, as part of your argument.
- Aim at coming to a synthesis between the sources and your own knowledge.
- Come to an independent judgement that you can sustain; it must be more than a simple assertion.

(b)   Using the evidence of all the sources and your own knowledge, how far would you agree with the view that it was lack of support from the newly enfranchised electorate of 1918 that explains the decline of the Liberal Party?   (40)

How to answer this question

Your approach to this question will be very similar to that for question (a), and all the points made in connection with your answer to question (a) will be relevant. There are, however, some differences that you must consider:

- Consider all the sources and work out how you will use them as building blocks in your argument.
- Remember to consider them as sources of evidence, not as sources of information.
- Plan your line of argument, remembering that you are dealing with an interpretation that you must support or refute. If you refute the view that it was lack of support from the newly enfranchised electorate of 1918 that explains the decline of the Liberal Party, remember that you should present an alternative, supported explanation.

EPILOGUE

This book began in 1890, with Martha and George Crane and their four children Alice, Henry, Agnes and Rose. We left them somewhere in the 1920s. Henry had died long before, and the three girls had their adult life before them. Martha and George were looking forward to an easier life – possibly even retirement now there were state pensions – with no dependent children and a little more money in their pockets. What happened to all of them?

Martha and George were not to have the retirement together for which they hoped. George, returning home from an evening at the local pub (drunk, some say) at the height of the General Strike in 1926, was knocked down and killed by a bus driven by a student strike-breaker. Martha was to live on for twenty more years, through the Second World War. She saw the birth of four great-grandchildren and watched them ride bikes, join the Brownies and listen to Children's Hour on the radio – all unheard of when Martha herself was a child.

Alice married William who was an inventor, a small time farmer and a man to take up any enterprise, no matter how unsound, with enthusiasm. They owned and lived on a farm in Northamptonshire. Their children Dorothy, Alfred and Norah went to private, fee paying schools in times of prosperity and the local village school when cash was short. The children's ponies, along with Alice's pony and trap, were sold to raise money and bought back again three times in as many years. Eventually facing bankruptcy, Alice and William were saved from disgrace by the rest of the family and went to live in a small cottage on the edge of the estate they once owned. William died just before the Second World War broke out in 1939. Alice was to live on for another thirty years, seeing the death of one daughter and the births of four grandchildren.

Agnes married Albert, who was half-Jewish and working his way steadily up through the ranks of the Post Office. Starting as a telegraph boy, he retired in 1934 as head sorter at the central London sorting office. He and Agnes lived in Willesden, London, moving to Kensal Rise when he was promoted in 1922. Their first child, Leonard, died when he was a baby, but their two daughters Elsie and Constance, lived long lives. Albert and Agnes moved out of London during the Second World War in order to avoid the blitz but moved back again as soon as the war ended. Rose went to live with them then and had her own room at the back of the house. Agnes died in the 1960s.

Rose never married. A talented seamstress, she worked as a machinist and, when she got bored with respectable work, took off and did a range of exciting and sometimes fairly dubious jobs, one of which was working as a fortune teller at the end of Brighton pier. She had a string of boyfriends, one of whom was William, Alice's husband. But the three sisters had a strong relationship that survived such betrayals. Rose lived with both her sisters: with Alice when she was widowed and then with Agnes and Albert, living beyond Albert's death and sitting with Agnes as she died. Rose was an avid bingo-player in later life, where a win of £100 took her on a weekend spree, aged 80, back to Brighton. 'What's life about', she would say, 'if you can't have a bit of fun on the way?'

BIBLIOGRAPHY

Many books have been written on the history of Britain between the years 1890 and 1939. Some are general accounts and some deal with specific topics in depth. The following are particularly useful:

AS SECTION: BRITAIN 1890–1939

Paul Adelman, *The Rise of the Labour Party 1880–1945* (Longman, 1972)

Paul Adelman, *The Decline of the Liberal Party 1910–1931* (Longman, 1981)

Paul Adelman, *Great Britain and the Irish Question 1800–1922* (Hodder & Stoughton, 1996)

Stuart Ball, *The Conservative Party and British Politics 1902–1951* (Longman, 1995)

Paula Bartley, *Votes for Women 1860–1928* (Hodder & Stoughton, 1998)

Robert Blake, *The Decline of Power 1915–64* (Granada, 1985)

Peter Clarke, *Hope and Glory: Britain 1900–1990* (Penguin, 1996)

R.A. Florey, *The General Strike of 1926* (Calder, 1980)

Keith Laybourn, *The Rise of Labour* (Edward Arnold, 1988)

Arthur Marwick, *The Deluge: British Society and the First World War* (Bodley Head, 1965)

Kenneth O. Morgan, *Lloyd George* (Weidenfeld & Nicolson, 1974)

Margaret Morris, *The General Strike* (Penguin, 1976)

C.L. Mowat, *Britain between the Wars* (Methuen, 1974)

Robert Pearce, *Domestic Politics 1918–39* (Hodder & Stoughton, 1992)

Martin Pugh, *The Making of Modern British Politics 1867–1939* (Blackwell, 1982)

Martin Pugh, *State and Society 1870–1997* (Arnold, 1994)

Donald Read, *Edwardian England 1901–15* (Harrap, 1972)

A.J.P. Taylor, *English History 1914–45* (Penguin, 1970)

Andrew Thorpe, *Britain in the 1930s* (Blackwell, 1992)

Andrew Thorpe, *The History of the British Labour Party* (Macmillan, 1997)

Kenneth Young, *Baldwin* (Weidenfeld & Nicholson, 1976)

A2 SECTION: THE DECLINE OF THE LIBERAL PARTY

George Bernstein, *Liberalism and Liberal Politics in Edwardian England* (Allen & Unwin, 1981)

P.E. Clarke, *Lancashire and the New Liberalism* (CUP, 1971)

George Dangerfield, *The Strange Death of Liberal England* (Constable, 1935)

Edward David, 'The Liberal Party divided 1916–1918', *The Historical Journal*, 13 (1970)

Roy Gregory, *The Miners and British Politics 1906–14* (OUP, 1968)

Michael Hart, 'The Liberals, the War and the Franchise', *English Historical Review*, 97 (1982)

Michael Lynch, *Lloyd George and the Liberal Dilemma* (Hodder & Stoughton, 1993)

H.C.G. Matthew, R.I. McKibbin and J.A. Kay, 'The Franchise Factor in the Rise of the Labour Party', *English Historical Review*, 261 (1976)

Ross McKibbin, *The Evolution of the Labour Party 1910–24* (OUP, 1974)

Kenneth O. Morgan, *Consensus and Disunity: The Lloyd George Coalition 1918–22* (Clarendon Press, 1979)

Henry Pelling, 'Labour and the Downfall of Liberalism', in *Popular Politics and Society in late Victorian Britain* (Macmillan, 1968)

D. Tanner, *Political Change and the Labour Party 1900–18* (CUP, 1990)

D. Tanner, 'The Parliamentary Electoral System, the "Fourth" Reform Act, and the Rise of Labour in England and Wales', *Bulletin of the Institute of Historical Research* (1976)

T. Wilson, *The Downfall of the Liberal Party* (Fontana, 1968)

SOURCE BOOKS

Lawrence Butler and Harriet Jones (eds), *Britain in the Twentieth Century: A Documentary Reader: vol. 1, 1900–1939* (Heinemann, 1994)

John Gorman, *To Build Jerusalem* (Scorpion, 1980)

Keith Laybourn, *Modern Britain since 1906: A Reader* (Tauris, 1999)

FICTION

Walter Greenwood, *Love on the Dole* (1933)

George Orwell, *The Road to Wigan Pier* (1937)

Charles Petrie, *Scenes of Edwardian Life* (1965)

Maud Pemberton Reeves, *Round about a Pound a Week* (Virago, 1979)

R. Tressell, *The Ragged Trousered Philanthropists* (Grafton, 1965)

INDEX

To help you get the grades you deserve at AS and A-level History you'll need up-to-date books that cover exactly the right topics and help you at exam time.

So that's precisely what we've written.

The Heinemann Advanced History Series

15th - 18th Century

Spain 1474-1700
0 435 32733 X

The English Reformation: Crown Power and Religous Change, 1485-1558
0 435 32712 7

The European Reformation: 1500-1610
0 435 32710 0

The Reign of Elizabeth
0 435 32735 6

The Coming of the Civil War: 1603-49
0 435 32713 5

England in Crisis: 1640-60
0 435 32714 3

France in Revolution: 1776-1830
0 435 32732 1

The Reign of Henry VII 1450-1509
0 435 32742 9

Oliver Cromwell
0 435 32756 9

France 1500-1715
0 435 32751 8

19th - 20th Century: British

Britain 1815-51: Protest and Reform
0 435 32716 X

Poverty & Public Health: 1815-1948
0 435 32715 1

The Extension of the Franchise: 1832-1931
0 435 32717 8

Liberalism and Conservatism 1846-1905
0 435 32737 2

European Diplomacy 1870-1939
0 435 32734 8

British Imperial and Foreign Policy 1846-1980
0 435 32753 4

Britain 1890-1939
0 435 32757 7

Britain 1929-1998
0 435 32738 0

19th - 20th Century: European

Russia 1848-1917
0 435 32718 6

Lenin and the Russian Revolution
0 435 32719 4

Stalinist Russia
0 435 32720 8

Germany 1848-1914
0 435 32711 9

Germany 1919-45
0 435 32721 6

Mussolini and Italy
0 435 32725 9

The Modernisation of Russia 1856-1985
0 435 32741 0

Italian Unification 1820-71
0 435 32754 2

European Diplomacy 1890-1939
0 435 32734 8

20th Century: American and World

Civil Rights in the USA 1863-1980
0 435 32722 4

The USA 1917-45
0 435 32723 2

The Cold War - Conflict in Europe and Asia
0 435 32736 4

Heinemann

Inspiring generations

tel 01865 888080   fax 01865 314029   email orders@heinemann.co.uk   web www.heinemann.co.uk